Rungli-Rungliot

{Thus Far and No Further}

Rungli-Rungliot

{Thus Far and No Further}

a memoir

RUMER GODDEN

Foreword by
RUSKIN BOND

SPEAKING
TIGER

SPEAKING TIGER BOOKS LLP
125 A, Shahpur Jat, Near Asiad Village
New Delhi–110049, India

First published by Peter Davies, London, 1944
First published in India in paperback by Speaking Tiger 2015

For sale in the Indian subcontinent only.

ISBN: 978-93-85288-39-5
eISBN: 978-93-85288-40-1

10 9 8 7 6 5 4 3 2

Typeset in Adobe Jenson Pro by Jojy Philip, New Delhi
Printed at Chaman Enterprises, New Delhi

To Jon

and the spirit of little Joss,

who was born here

The Place remote—their coats and scarves old,
The year fruitful—their talk and laughter gay.

CHINESE POEM
(Translated by Arthur Waley)

There are only a few things in these notes:

Chinglam and its hills and valleys
Work
Flowers
Children
Animals
Servants

There is nothing else because there
was nothing else.

RUMER GODDEN

FOREWORD

After a gap of sixty-five years, it's great to come back to a book that gave me so much pleasure when I first read it.

In the year 1952 I was alone and friendless on the island of Jersey, in the Channel Islands between France and England. And I was homesick, longing for the friends and happy times I'd left behind in my little corner of India. Twice a week I'd visit the local library, and here one day I discovered this little book, *Rungli-Rungliot ('Thus Far and No Further')*, Rumer Godden's charming, evocative journal of a year spent in another little corner of India, the tea-gardens on the Himalayan slopes below Darjeeling. It took me back to my own Himalayan slopes—above Dehradun—and gave me a feeling of hope and reassurance at a time when I was badly in need of both.

Rumer Godden was a gifted and sensitive writer who had just made a name for herself with her memorable novel *Black Narcissus*, set in a convent near Darjeeling. A few years later it was turned into a film starring Deborah Kerr, Jean Simmons, and Sabu. But at the time it was written, Rumer Godden was in financial difficulties, deserted by a fickle husband and forced to give ballroom-dancing lessons in wartime Calcutta.

The year in the tea-estate offered her some respite, enabling her to work at her next novel and bring up her two small daughters.

Black Narcissus became a critical and commercial success, as did her other novels set in pre-Partition India—*The River* and *Breakfast with the Nikolides*. In 1951, *The River* became a lyrical and visually beautiful film directed by Jean Renoir, the great French director.

I read *The River* after the film was released in a Jersey cinema, and once again I was transported back to India—so much so, that I saw the film several times during its brief run on the island. Not only did it make me a lifelong fan of Rumer Godden's book and Jean Renoir's films, but it helped me to complete the novel, my first, that I was working on at the time; for I too wanted to capture, or recapture, some of the timeless beauty, the soul of the India I'd left behind.

Rumer Godden and her sister Jon Godden wrote many successful novels, short-story collections and memoirs, but it is their early 'Indian' oeuvre that remains fresh and still enjoyable today, and I am happy that some of these books are being republished in the country that inspired them.

Ruskin Bond
Landour, Mussoorie
June 2015

Rungli-Rungliot

{Thus Far and No Further}

Rungli-Rungliot.

All that I have left of it are these pages of notes and some lemon leaves that I put between them; the leaves are brittle now and will soon dry into dust but they still have a scent. It is not long since I picked them, but days and happenings and changes have widened into a gulf. I remember—but I am forgetting; forgetting the exact small things. I am forgetting the sound of the prayer flags in the wind on the ridge that stood up into the sky, where the Rungli-Rungliot Lama might have walked and meditated as I liked to walk and think; and I am forgetting the sound of the flute that played in the dusk as I was coming home; and the sight of the clouds blowing off the snows, and the wild cherry trees, and the sunflowers tumbling down the hill and the coolie women stooping to marvel at Sabrina's feet, small and green-white as lilies, as she paddled in the stream.

I am forgetting; but when I smell the lemon leaves I am back again. They seem to distil Chinglam. To distil? That is to extract the spirit or essential oil. That is what I want these notes to do.

Rungli-Rungliot, means in Paharia 'thus far and no further'.

Once upon a time, perhaps when Noah lived and perhaps this flood was Noah's flood too, in another time when the earth was filled with violence, the waters of the Teesta river in North Bengal, India, began to rise in the valleys of the Himalayas, whose ranges are higher and more terrible than the Andes. The water rose higher and higher, past the foot hills and the low hills, past the villages of Riyang and Teesta Bazaar, until it reached to the spurs nearly at the top of the mountains and the people began to be seriously afraid that their retreat would be cut off by the sky. I think only the spines of the ridges showed in the water, spines of monsters and dragons petrified, with their colours hidden in the Teesta that today, after the rains, is that same milky blue. The prayer flags were snatched and carried to the ridge, the horns blew and the drums sounded, while behind and inaccessible, the line of snows that not even a flood could reach, reared themselves into the sky.

Down below them the consternation continued and the water spread and rose and spread.

In a temple at the top of one of these ridges, a Lama was saying his prayers. The people went in and disturbed him, but they disturbed him quietly; the horns stopped blowing, the drums were not beaten, and the people were still as their headmen went in to him.

'Well, what is it?' said the Lama.

'The water—the water is coming up.' It was. The people were standing in it; it was lapping the temple steps.

'Tell it to go down,' said the Lama.

'*Tell* it?'

'Yes. Give it a positive order.'

'But—it won't pay any attention.'

'Won't it?' said the Lama. 'Then I must tell it myself.' And he came out from his prayers and put out his hand.

I think of him as looking Chinese in a stiff robe, with a Chinese absorbed and peaceful face. He looked at the spines of the hills and the water swirling round them and the jumbled colours of the people and their frightened faces and silent horns and agitated flags; he looked up at the sky and the unmoving snows and back at the water, and he put out his hand and said, 'Rungli Rungliot. Thus far and no further.'

The flood immediately stopped; the water went down and the Lama went back to his prayers.

The words that he said, stayed there in the place as its name.

Rungli-Rungliot is a real place on the spur of the Himalayas, facing south above the plains and the gorge of the little Runglee river that they say was left behind by accident when the Teesta water fell. Rungli-Rungliot is now a post and telegraph office and a police out-post; it serves eight tea estates. It has two small white-washed buildings in hedges of poinsettia, two policemen, a post-office clerk and a very old peon who delivers telegrams at a crawl. Every afternoon the runners come in from the tea gardens with locked leather

satchels on their backs to which the post-clerk babu has the key; he unlocks the bags, takes out the post and puts in the day's mail that has come by another runner from Darjeeling; he locks the bag again and sends the runners off. Some of them come in twelve miles every day.

I had a runner too and Rungli-Rungliot was my postal address; I stayed seven miles below it at Chinglam, the out-bungalow of Rungolo Tea Estate, for a winter unique in beauty, humour and joy. This was surprising, as when I went there I had no expectation of anything, particularly not of joy.

It was wartime; I was threatened by trouble; but all the time I was there I seemed to be living under the protection of that little yellow hand.

THERE WERE THREE addresses: What did I know about them? What did I know between them? Only that they were all on the same tea-garden though they were several miles apart; that they had been, even when they were lived in, rather ramshackle; that they were all unbelievably beautiful. The assistants who had lived in them had gone to the war, these remote bungalows were to let to anyone who liked mountains and clouds and spaces and loneliness. They were all empty.

I LEFT CALCUTTA to see them on a July night in a train that rolled and groaned northwards across Bengal until the morning, when it left me at a little town on the edge of a forest that dripped with rain. I took another train, like the train in an Amusement Park, and puffed away through the trees up the foothills of the Himalayas. The trees dripped, the hanging orchids dripped, the creepers dripped, the banks at the edge of the track dripped and the carriage dripped inside as well as out. We crept along at the edge of the Teesta river, up the valley, and the river looked as if it might flood again; it was wide and deep and incredibly swift, neither green nor grey in the rain swell but celadon, between low banks of grey white stones all made smooth by the water. After the rains, in the winter, the river would be blue; first a chalky blue and then a blue with a grape-green tinge from the ice water. It is a dangerous cruel river, as cruel as it is beautiful, and the hill people say it has to take a life a year.

Each side of it the gorge goes up to the mountains and, at the far end, they part to show the snow peak, Kabru.

The little train stopped and started and made an amount of smoke and an amount of noise far beyond its size. The engine had a high, flat-topped funnel and bulging coal bunkers, it was painted a spinach-green and a coolie stood on the ledge in front of it as we went along; occasionally he stepped off and walked. The first- and second-class carriages were empty and the third-class carriages were so full that people sat on the window ledges, on the luggage, on each other, and luggage and children and hens oozed out of the corners and openings. All along the train, blowing into my window as I sat solitary in state, was an overpowering smell of *biris*; a biri is a little evil-smelling cigarette rolled in its natural leaf; every hill man, woman or child, smokes them.

After a great many hours the train crossed a red bridge over another river with deep fish pools, looped the loop, and arrived panting at my station, that was a collection of tin-roofed huts in the middle of the forest; but it had a station-master in full uniform with a whistle and a green flag, and a small-size grey car that had come to meet me and drive me twelve miles on a hairpin track up the precipices and gorges of the mountain to the tea estate.

W. WAS THE manager of the tea estate, and W. took me to see the houses.

They were spread out along the ridge of the mountain, with the valley below and Rungli-Rungliot above; the factory and the manager's house, W.'s house, were in the centre. The valley was between the folds of the mountains that folded back on themselves, higher and higher, blue towards their tips and streaked with waterfalls. The Runglee river lay in the bottom of the valley, and often, now in the rains, it was covered with clouds, and clouds lay across the mountains in isolated fantastic shapes.

The first bungalow, the Little Bungalow, was small and new, close beside the factory and near W.'s house; it was accessible, it had electric light, it was not lonely; but the rooms were little and dark and they were filled with the skins, the mounted heads and skulls and bones of the animals its former owner had shot. They would all have to be cared for and I did not think I should like dusting dead tiger heads.

The second house was Rungjeli, far up against the hill at the head of the valley with a wonderful view to the plains. To reach it we crossed a suspension bridge hung in space above a precipice, a bridge that swung and bounced and quivered under us. The house was built close up against the hill and the rankness and earth smell of the close thickets and grass was in every room; the view opened in front of us, but there was a smell of old earth and decay and softening wood and the rain had made streaks of green down the walls. There was a perpetual soft dripping and creaking and a falling-down of dust.

W. All that can be made right, you know.

'But, W., look!' High up in the eaves of the verandah were hundreds of red paper tags on strings.

'*Bats?*' W. nodded.

W.—after a minute. No, I suppose it wouldn't do.

The road to the third house was a scratch along the ridges of the mountain with nothing to edge it; it was just wide enough to hold the car; its corners cut clear into the sky; we had to reverse round some of those corners and the drop below was more than a thousand feet. I emphasize this road because the menace of it was always between us and the outside world; the fear endured on it always made the arrival at Chinglam more than ever pleasant.

W. drove on, in and out of streams, up perpendicular banks, while the pebbles rolled from our wheels and bounced into the gulf. We rounded gorges and glades of bamboos interspaced with plantations of tea; when we came into the tea I breathed again, because the bushes looked sturdy and comfortable. We passed earth coolie huts built on shelves along the hill, and the people and the children ran out to look at us; the boys laughed, the girls looked at us more seriously and the little ones ran after the car until they fell down, when they did not cry, but lay on their stomachs in the dust still looking. Round corners we came suddenly on pack ponies carrying panniers of tea-leaf and their drivers snatched at their heads and turned them to the hill and we edged past their tails. Terraces of tea spread above us, and below, far below, were bamboos and coolie crops. The car screamed in first gear up a hill like a wall, struggling, screaming, while we all leant forward and did not dare to breathe.

The road made one more tremendous climb and ran out, with a curious gentleness, on to a white drive among the tea bushes that was Chinglam.

Chinglam is the out-bungalow of the garden where once, before the war, the senior assistant lived, inhabiting the house when he was not away working or shooting or visiting.

Chinglam is the last section of the garden and the house is on a knoll. I do not know how else to describe it, it is so gentle, but the knoll is thousands of feet high and sits above the clouds, and from the lawn it looks down over the tops of the trees and the tea to the river. It looks up to the mountains and away to the plains that make a faint map to the East, and in the valley that morning the clouds lay in the exact shape of the Chinese character for heaven.

The house is an island entirely surrounded by tea; the tea goes down below to the river with zigzag paths cutting it into sharp patterns, and the bushes make a pattern of dark green on pale green undergrowth and the shade trees spread above them like dull green lace. The tea goes up above with more zigzags to a crest of bamboos where the ridge cuts the sky, the ridge we call the Saddle where the Lama may have walked. The saddle looks north to Kalimpong and Rinchinpong and the Sikkim snows, and a path leads away from it along the spine of the mountain to the View Point where we go to see the big snows, the Kanchenjunga range.

Tea spreads away again to the East where the mountains open, and, on fine days, show the Teesta river winding in the plains; and it spreads back to the West past the bungalows and factory to the waterfall at Rungjeli. Opposite on mountains rearing themselves against the sky are the buildings and nurseries of the Chincona Plantation; the houses look clear and tiny, the wooden rows of nursery huts for the young quinine look like honeycombs, and the plantations of trees are only blurs of green on the mountain side.

When I first saw it that morning Chinglam house sat on the knoll against the hill, but not too near it; it was a large, shabby, white-washed house with the paint peeling off the verandah posts and a red roof that came low to the ground. It had the quality of a good house though it was old; it was dry and had wide windows and wide fireplaces for wood fires. There were only four rooms, high with white ceilings and white-washed walls, but it had a big verandah and big bathrooms. Inside it smelled of wood just sawn, which is what it was patched with, and outside it smelled of roses and lemon trees and jasmine and growing tea.

The garden was mostly green and I like green gardens. I walked up and down the little rough lawn that had a path to one side where lemon trees grew; on the borders of the lawn were beds full of a strange mixture of bushes and flowers and weeds; unpruned roses, orchids, zinnias and wild coffee that has thick white flowers the shape of stars.

W. left me to make up my mind. On the edge of the lawn was the gong for calling the coolies in and, as I stood there, an old old man came out and rang it and the sound of it floated across the valley. He took no notice of me and the sound of the gong echoed back to him from the mountain on the other side. That was the only sound, that and the sound of the streams. It was very quiet and quite alone. I listened to the streams and thought.

Can I live here alone, with the mists and the rain and the silence, when the waterfall at the head of the valley miles away will make a roar in the night and the streams will sound loudly all day long? There will be no one but the Chinese-faced coolies with their old clothes and soft indistinct speaking; no one but the children because I do not think our governess, Giovanna, will stay; there will be no one but the children and the servants and the dogs. W. and his wife live at the other end of the valley, and they have busy lives; I cannot expect to get to Darjeeling more than once in a long while; I am melancholy and nervous. Can I bear it? And as I thought, I had a feeling as if I had escaped; a feeling of release or, if it could not be as much as that, of reprieve.

I looked at the house again. There was none of the dreariness of Rungjeli, none of the fright I expected to find, so isolated and away. Chinglam has the gentleness I marked as we first came to it, and a beauty of space and cloud and water and the wild deep colours of the mountain. Then, in the rains, the colours were sodden green with the growth of the monsoon; dark green tea, pale and dark bamboos, pale grasses, brilliant patches of millet, and the colours were heavily streaked with white of waterfalls and clouds. Later in the winter, W. said, the mountains would be blue with a wild harebell blueness and the waterfalls would narrow to a thread and the river be ice-green without rapids, and every shadow and leaf and twig and bud would stand out in clear sun.

So I looked at it with that feeling of release in my mind, and up the path to me came W.

W. Well, do you like it? Do you want to stay?

'Yes,' I said slowly, 'I want to stay.'

We come to Chinglam on the first Sunday in August. We are: Rafael who is five, Sabrina who is three, Giovanna who is twenty-six, and I. We also have with us Ears, our Lepcha manservant, and Ayah, his wife, and their three little girls; our sweeper Kokil, and four pekinese, Sol and young Sol and Comfort and Candytuft who is young and very small and white and rare.

We have our first tea sitting on the bare verandah among the boxes. The garden is in sun after rain, with raindrops in the blades and on the leaves and flowers and drops shining and falling on the trees. The lawn ends in clouds that are sweeping below it.

Sabrina. Why the sky has come down here?

Rafael. Silly, we have come up to the sky.

Giovanna, with a sigh of bliss. I feel me to be in Switzerland.

I look at them and it seems to me that I have not seen them for a long time. I thought I knew them intimately, but they are strangers. Giovanna is pouring out tea in my place and now I remember that I have only been a visitor at teatime. The three of them talk and joke and some of the jokes are family and private and I do not understand them. Rafael, sitting up to the table, is not the plump baby I have been thinking she is; she is not plump and she is not a baby, she is a slim little girl with an erect back and red-gold hair and eyes that are full of dreams and thoughts; thoughtful eyes. I cannot see Sabrina's eyes; I can only see her eyebrows, level with the table; they are two crescents of eyebrows, black and delicate and curiously mature. Sabrina does not seem to have seen me either; every time I speak the eyebrows turn in my direction.

I feel suddenly discouraged. I get up and go down the steps into the garden, and I walk up and down the lawn with the drops wetting my shoes and a smell of wet earth and greenness in my nostrils that are still dry and full of town dust. What have I been doing this last year? I try to think and I do not know. I have been like a squirrel in a cage going round and round without any sense of direction, seeing nothing, missing everything. I can remember nothing of anything except my own work and that must have been the only time I came down from the wheel on to the floor. I stand still looking at the chasing clouds and I feel as if a mist were rolling off my mind as well.

I stand still and Chinglam is still too; there is no movement except the movement of the clouds; even the leaves are still. The sense of hurry and press is slipping away; the hours of this afternoon have spun themselves out into a length that promises that the days will all come round evenly and long. Will they get too long? Will they lengthen into an interminable dragging time because of this stillness? This emptiness? But the emptiness is of the Buddhist kind, an emptiness of space and not of blankness; already I have noticed that the time flows. Now it moves towards evening and bedtime, our first bedtime in this house.

I turn towards it. The voices of Rafael and Sabrina and Giovanna come to me distinctly, almost impressively, in the quiet.

THE EARS FAMILY arrive late. They and Kokil and the dogs, all but Candytuft who is spoiled, had to walk from the station. They come in with each little girl sitting on a pack pony with a dog in front of her. They have none of them walked as far for years and their Calcutta shoes are cut to pieces, but they arrive without depressions or complaints and with smiles.

Ears. It is like my country, like Sikkim.

Ayah. Like when we were young. Aie! It is good to feel the climate again.

I saw Ears first eleven years ago on a sunny morning in Darjeeling, and my impression of him has always been as bright and white as that day of sun on snow; snow: white clothes and teeth, sun: golden-brown face; added to this a little round hat and a smile. Even when he began to drink, even when he had cholera, my impression of Ears has not changed. We have had ups and downs with him, but only two downs and a great many ups.

To himself he has added Mrs Ears. I have never known quite what to do with Mrs Ears; she has not been needed, but now, when Giovanna goes, she will be needed at last. Mrs Ears, Ayah, is an avowed fool but she is a fine tidy gentle sensitive fool. Fine can mean 'not coarse or heavy, thin, slender, exquisite', though it can also mean 'splendid and showy'. Her fineness has the first meaning. She lends grace and sweetness to the house; she never bangs, she never flounces, she never tries to control or contradict anyone. She folds clothes into tidy little heaps, she arranges and dusts and puts things away in places where you can never find them, but it does not matter as she is always there to bring them to you. She pets the dogs and spoils the children, her own and mine.

She has added three little slit-eyed girls to the Ears family; they wear all the family wealth in necklaces of coins.

Kokil goes all round the house and his moustaches bristle.

Kokil. This is a very peculiar place. It is very wild and very dirty. You must buy me a long broom and a stick.

There are more servants waiting for them; a galaxy of servants.

'Do we need them *all?*' I say to W.

W. I think you will. This isn't like living in quite an ordinary place, you know.

They are not quite ordinary servants. There is a cook, and

a boy to wait at the table and a garden boy, but there is also a watchman, a woodcutter, a water-carrier, a washerman and a bread-runner. They are all hill people, Nepalis, so that the Ears family are at home with them, but Kokil is very much a foreigner. I introduce them to one another and they go to their own quarters, which are behind a hedge of poinsettias behind the house.

The first night is long and feels strange. My weariness seems to beat around the house in waves, but the little house is steady in the sleeping tea under the stars. I lie and listen to the sound of the waterfall; sometimes my thoughts come over it, sometimes its sound comes over my thoughts.

In the very early morning there is a smell of dew and a cock crows startlingly under my window.

Presently Ayah comes in with my tea. She says she has not slept either. In the night, Shoomi and Poori and Dicki, the little girls, howled in terror every time the jackals howled.

The first time I ever met W. was when he was an assistant and lived on another garden below Darjeeling. I went to tea with him and he had a python in his chicken run. It was a full-sized python but there was no need to be afraid, as he pointed out, because it was anchored in the middle by a deer that it had eaten, which was progressing, by degrees of slow digestion, towards its tail.

He had caught it when he was out shooting in the lower valleys and his coolies had carried it by branches, passed one over and one under it all the way up, and joined at the side as if it were carried between two ladders. No one but W. could have made the coolies do it, because it was very evil and very heavy.

'I wouldn't go *too* near it,' said W. 'It can smite a good blow with its head or its tail that would stun you or brain you.'

Its head was the most repulsive and the most wicked thing I had ever seen, shaped like a great pebble flattened on the top, with a horrible grey-green skin wrinkled into pouches under stony grey-green eyes. It seemed more saurian than snake.

Now that his assistants have gone to the war, W. runs this garden of two thousand five hundred acres by himself; a thousand acres of it is tea, the rest is forestry and coolie-cultivated, but all of it is under W. He covers it by relays of ponies now that petrol rationing has stopped his car, though sometimes he uses a motor-cycle that sounds loudly in these silent hills; the coolies call it his 'Putputti'.

W. is a birdman; he writes articles for magazines and Natural History Societies; there are few Himalayan birds that he does not know. He is a magnificent shot and though he has shot everything, even ibex in Kashmir, next to markhor the peak of endurance in shooting, he is as avid to shoot everything again. I have seldom seen anyone as completely well as W. The colour of his skin is almost tawny and I have never seen him tired. Not only is he strong, he is kind. The children worship him.

Very kind to me is M. his wife; with presents of flowers and fruit and vegetables, with recipes and wise advice she helps in any and every need. I am afraid I need a great deal of help, but M. does not get impatient, and to feel she is there at the other end of the telephone is strength to me. She has a beautiful house and garden that she keeps in an order I could never achieve. We can see the house across the valley.

Their prestige on the estate is enormous. He is king and she is queen and their power among the people is absolute. A less nice man would have become complicated, but W. is genuinely popular and full of a lordly happiness, all the happier and good to see because it is so lordly.

It does not take us long to settle. The very poorness of the rooms at Chinglam have a kind of beauty; there is so little in them that of themselves they achieve space and simplicity, things that are necessary in a house for me. The rooms all have large windows, white-washed walls, wooden floors and open log fires.

The bedrooms have only the beds and built-in cupboards of natural red wood; there is a dresser with a round wicker stool in mine and there is a tallboy in the children's. Mine has white rugs, white curtains faintly barred with blue, and Sikkim blankets on the beds in blue and cream and red and purple woven colours. In the wall vase above the fire where the mantel should be, Giovanna has put a bunch of nasturtiums and cornflowers and cherry-pie and white geranium; if I saw a bowl of Giovanna's flowers in paradise, where it would quite naturally go, I should say at once 'Giovanna Transpose.' The children's bedroom has a blue rug and blue curtains checked with white, red eiderdowns, and their red name hearts on their bed-heads. The day nursery is to match, with red painted furniture, many books and pictures and very few toys.

The verandah is half garden and half room; it is whitened along its edge and has a row of pots and flowers; orchids hang on its posts; it has green and white chairs and a saddlestand and compass points cut on the floor by someone who lived here before. We use one end as a dining-room and there the old estate table and chairs stand on a matting of red and green and cream.

The drawing-room is more furnished than any other room, but it only has a couch and two chairs of cane and wood and shelves for books along the wall. I brought my blue Tabriz hunting carpet, with flowers and leopards and deer in pale Persian colours; and I brought my blue Bristol glass bowls and my three-sized Nanking bowls; my books, a small curved table and cushions in faint colours that echo the carpet. It is a friendly happy room, full of firelight and flowers, and there are four baskets with willow-pattern cushions and, like another echo, over the fireplace is a picture of four pekinese in sepia and white and gold from the *Scroll of a Thousand Pekinese,* the stud book of the Emperor... These

things are the stamp by which I know my house is mine; they are a reassurance to me; they have been in all the houses I have had and turned them into homes.

I have an office leading off the drawing-room and there is a store-room leading out of that. Giovanna has a small room off the children's. The first thing she does is to take down the curtains. She has a Swiss passion for cleanliness and hygiene and a disregard of colour in a room. I hate curtains that go across the window and cut its panel in half, and I hate muffled windows, but I love curtains that have colours and blow, and these rooms are large and white like great white caves and the colours of the curtains break the whiteness up and rest your eyes; but Giovanna takes hers down. Every day she loops the children's curtains up out of sight and every day I shake them out and let them hang again. This battle has been going on a long time, ever since I have known Giovanna. Occasionally I speak to her about it and the curtains are allowed to hang—for a few days; sooner or later they are looped up again.

August 18th.

They say if a worm has been cut in half and you put the two ends into quiet earth in a flower pot and do not investigate, they will grow into as good a worm or better. Will that happen to me here?

The quiet is extraordinary. I find myself listening, waiting for something to happen. It has been raining, and the quiet is contained in the house. Giovanna disappears after breakfast with the children, housekeeping takes me hardly half-an-hour, and after that I am left with the day; there are no engagements, no duties, no fatigues. I feel as if hundreds of threads that were binding me, sewn painfully into me, tight and pulling, were breaking one by one. I had thought they were integral; I feel each one as it breaks, there is a pang and a sense of loss until it heals, but it does heal and I feel free.

Even the war seems to have receded. I did not ask for this, but we have no wireless and our paper is two days old when we get it. There is only work, and for the first time space to do it, and the children and the garden and the peculiar strangeness of this place.

I think of something I said to a friend when I told him I was coming to Chinglam.

'But what in the world will you do there?'

'Live there.'

'But what will you *do?*'

'Live.'

Then I did not know what I was saying.

I AM BEGINNING to know these new servants and to distinguish some of the coolies. They were delighted when they heard we were coming to live here, we were new and exciting to look at and knots of them are always gathered round a rock above the drive where they can see us.

There is somebody who is not pleased and that is the thin old man who came out to ring the gong that first day. He is Chinglam's familiar, the chowkidar, the caretaker of the house and tool sheds.

He is dirty, so old that in his face only the forehead is left clear, the rest is all deep wrinkles the colour of cedar wood. He is unbelievably smelly with a rich old smell; when he comes into the office to telephone I have to go out and open the door and window afterwards. His clothes were once white and now have every colour of earth and grass and smoke in them. He has cherished the bungalow for more than fifty years, seen it knocked down by the earthquake and built up again, seen the young assistants come and go away and come and go away. After each one he has been able to put the bungalow back exactly as it was before; now he can never do that again. Now, at the end of his life, I have come and irremediably changed it.

I have sent away old tables and chairs that he has known and kept through every stage of grease and dirt and rot; I have put the dining-room outside on the verandah and made the dining-room into a nursery and Chinglam has never had such a thing before. I have painted the furniture red and brought in strange furniture of my own and built in cupboards and shelves and book-shelves. I have thrown away his broken flower-pots and rusty kerosene tins planted with ferns on the verandah. I have fussed about the cleanliness of the servants' huts and ordered that pigs are not to be kept in the kitchen, and insisted that the rubbish is to be collected into a pit and burnt instead of being thrown down the bank in front of the house as it was so naturally and easily before.

He has not attempted to compete or to protest, he has simply accepted, but now he does not come into the house very much. His set occupation is to measure the rain, of which there is plenty, and telephone the result to the factory; he also gives out the tools to the coolies on the Chinglam section and theoretically he is in charge of the house whether I am here or not.

I have tried to conciliate him. I have asked his advice and made the servants show him respect. Now, when he sees me in the morning he gives me a peculiar, reverent and quavering salaam, an arm across his chest, the elbow of the other resting on the palm and its palm touching his forehead.

The servants call him Baju, grandfather. He is not a nice old man, he is tyrannical; he bullies the garden-boy and scolds him for picking a rose, one on a bush that is overgrown with damp pink windblown roses.

August 19th.

The rains go on. We have had six days' rain without stopping, six days walled in the house with white driving mist. We cannot see the chincona mountain at all. The children and Giovanna go out and come back beaten and gasping and sodden with rain, and Ayah puts their coats to dry on a topper, a huge wicker-work top like a mushroom over a pan of hot charcoal. The house smells of mould and wet wool. I found the soles of all my shoes covered with fungus.

The garden servants wear wicker shields on their backs and heads and the coolies wear them too and look like tortoises as they pluck the tea; twice W. has had to ring the gong at midday to call them in, it was too saturating even for them.

This is not as depressing as it sounds. The constant drumming noise on the tin roof has something steady and soothing about it; if it began and left off and began again I should find it nerve-racking, but it seems inevitable and my nerves accept it. The house seems like a fort held against the wet and mist and the fires are cheerful now that W. has sent us two ponyloads of dry wood from the factory. At night, lying in bed, and watching the fire and listening to the rain, I go to sleep and stay asleep and have no dreams.

Pink is a precious colour and should never be used in quantities. The Chinese are the people that understand that best. There should be a little, a very little in every room. My Nanking bowls give it to my room, three of them, big, middle-sized, little, of a faint Chinese pink with flowers and people enamelled on them. The Nanking bowls give it to my room and I repeat it usually in the linings of the curtains; there is an exact faint wisp of the colour in my Persian hunting carpet, where leopards and deer are hunted in a world of turquoise blue.

I shall always have pale walls and white rugs, and I hope I shall have wood fires, and I want good bread, good coffee and good salads and, if there is a garden at all, I hope it will be green, like this one; a green garden and reasonably old.

I have these things at Chinglam; my carpet, my books and bowls and the pekinese picture are here, but they are voyagers like I am, they give me no feeling of permanence. I am beginning to like Chinglam, but I have no expectation of being allowed to stay here whether I want to—or not.

THE WAR ITSELF has so placed me that I am out of it—for a while at any rate. My knitting is more of an impediment than a help and there is nothing else I can do here. L. has gone, Giovanna will go, I have to look after and support two children. I have to do that and work and save as much of everything as I can. There is nothing else, just now, to do.

Then I must ration worry. The Buddhists here put their prayer flags where the wind will blow them and their prayer wheels in the streams where the water will turn them and get on with their work while the prayers are said.

I think that is wisdom.

RAFAEL CAN READ to herself.

Rafael. Yes. I can do reading without talking.

I remember, a long time ago, when she first announced her intention of learning to do this, I wrote her a letter.

> You see, when you learn to read you will be born again into another world and it is a pity to be born again so young. I should put off reading, if I were you. As soon as you learn to read you will not see anything again quite as it is. It will all the time be altered by what you have read and you will also never be quite alone again. I should stay by yourself a bit longer if I were you.

Now she has learnt in spite of me, and so she always will do things in spite of, and occasionally because of, me. I ask her if she remembers the letter.

Rafael. Yes, but you wrote that when I was four. *Then* I used to paint prams upside down, *now* I can really paint. I am five.

She can paint. Her painting is remarkable and I wonder if this will last. Sabrina is remarkable herself; the most noisy difficult cantankerous contrary passionate child, as fragile as a wisp and as strong as an eel. They used to tell me she was a Cornish changeling; she was born at my home in Cornwall, a fair, transparent-skinned, blue-veined child amongst all the Cornish darkness. She seems more fair than ever here and all the coolies stop to look at her.

THE DOGS HAVE decided that they like the house. Now they possess it.

Everywhere I go—sit—stand—pause for a moment—there is a pekinese. They lie in whiting shapes, nose to tail, round me as I write. Their coats are beautiful, except young Sol, who is a very skimped pekinese with scarcely any feathers, paws the colour of cream cheese and a little oilcloth nose that is utterly shameful: it is brown. Young Sol is cheerfully unaware of how hideous he is and the dogs in the *Scroll* look down on him and prove that a thousand years ago brown noses were generally worn; three out of the four of the pekinese there are wearing them. Sol and Comfort and Candy are beautiful.

Sol, the elderly, has long ears with darkened tips and the colours of his coat run from cream through gold to raven, and his face is almost tortoise-shell. Comfort is plump, magnolia-coloured cream and white, with dark dark eyes and nose; she has on her forehead the decoration that the Chinese breeders prized more than any other in their dogs, it is between the eyes, a Little Ball Shining like Snow, a White Spot Leading to Heaven, and it portends the Jade Button in Front of the Hat, ambitions to be fulfilled.

The small Candytuft is not a dog, he is a fritillary, belonging to the butterfly family.

August 20th.

We have visitors. Henry, who is five, and his fat waddling Ayah, have come to stay with us.

The Ayah, Lena, is a Nepali by birth, but of low caste and, like many Indians who feel themselves inferior, she has become Christian. She dresses in a sari, though her native dress was a skirt and she carries a palm-leaf fan and wears ruby ear-rings and high-heeled shoes. She is a very efficient Ayah and is paid a large wage.

Ears and my Ayah look at the shoes and look at me.

'Lena, you must take off your shoes in the house.'

Lena. I am Christian, madam.

'You are also an Indian, Lena, and it is the Indian custom not to wear shoes in the house.'

Two glances like daggers from two beady little eyes sunk in fat cheeks. She goes and drops the shoes over the edge of the verandah.

August 21st.

Already the house is at peace and I have what I wanted most, a real office to work in. It was the assistant's office and it is furnished with a desk, a clock and a safe. As I sit in it I can see through the window up the side of the hill to the Saddle, past the drive bamboos and palms and the corner of the wicker stable and the bougainvillea that grows by it. The bougainvillea is the common kind, a bright magenta purple and its flowers as I see them in the frame of the window with the green bank behind them are vividly satisfying.

Get along then, work, run along your lines. Mount your train or you will never arrive at the terminus.

JUST AS I start work Giovanna comes to the door.

Giovanna. I disturb you—not?

I see something is burning that has to be said, and I sigh and tell her to come in.

A letter from Switzerland is in her hand, with a thin envelope chequered inside and covered with thin crisscrossed writing. It has one of the blue Swiss stamps of a blue Swiss landscape that fascinate Rafael.

'You have a letter from home?'

Giovanna, with a rush. My step-sister, she is married! To the Postmaster of—! And my friend Teresa, she is married too, and my cousin Tilde. I was like eldest sister to those. *She looks up at me in appeal.* I was the eldest sister.

We are both silent. We know what must be said. I should

have said it before we came here. Giovanna must go where she will have a chance to be in the world.

Giovanna is from Swiss Italy. She comes from a village on the shores of Lake Locarno, where her father built a house on the side that gets the least sun because it was cheaper.

Giovanna cannot remember her mother; she has a stepmother who sent her to be brought up in an orphanage by nuns so cruel, so vivid and so melodramatic that we can never hear enough stories about them; Giovanna's eyes flash as she tells about them and ours all flash in sympathy. Next she worked as something between a handyman, a slave, a tweeny and a machine for families in Switzerland, until she ran away and became a barmaid in an hotel in Zurich. Yes, truly, my children's governess is an ex-barmaid and a very delightful one too, and one most skilled and kind. The hotel sent her to England to learn English, and she became, as she says, nostalgic for small children and left her post of parlour-maid and came to me. She is a lovable, appreciative, sensible and attractive girl, very, very fond of the children and very, very fond of food. She works quite naturally from morning to night. We live together and yet manage to live apart and have learned to slip in and out of one another's lives with an easiness that I bless.

Now I say, 'Giovanna, listen to me.'

But she cannot listen. 'My *step-sister*, madam!'

August 25th.

It rained for six more days and now it has stopped. I go out to walk in the garden. The children are having tea and I can see the lamp shining on the wet bushes.

The rim of the hills is black against a sombre cloud-driven sky, but the valley is bright with a long beam of light that makes it deeply brilliantly green with one cloud across it.

This garden lifts up into the sky like a little plateau; the trees rise, not against a landscape, but against the sky. The grass and the leaves and bushes are colourless in the dark, but the white flowers shine, and the white pekinese; I cannot see the brown ones at all, nor the coloured flowers.

At the top of the drive is a rock where the coolie children sit to catch a glimpse of us. I sit there and two coolie girls pass me with baskets on their backs; the baskets are shaped like ice-cream cones and the girls' skirt pleats fall in front in folds to their bare feet. One smokes and the other sings, a high nasal little folk song that matches the dusk and the dark bushes and the small home sounds from the village down below in the valley.

They are friendly sounds. I want to know these people, not stay as an alien behind the white drive and the garden of Chinglam. When I am with W. they look at me as they talk to him, but if I am alone they part silently to let me pass. They do not speak Hindustani and I do not speak Paharia; the only one of us who can is Henry, but he is too shy to speak to them for us. There seems an enormous, insurmountable difference between us.

Tonight it is easier. The smoking girl takes her biri between her finger and thumb and puts it behind her and stays a moment; she looks at her feet and breathes through her nose and says 'salaam'. The other copies her. I smile at them and they smile at me and they go singing away towards the village and presently the song ends.

I FEEL INTENSELY about Henry because he is not mine. I feel very responsible for him far away like this. He is a thin little boy and when he is undressed his two shoulder-blades stand out like wings and, with his rather large head and curly hair and vague beautiful eyes, he looks like a cherub.

Rafael bullies him.

'But if Rafael hits you, Henry, you must hit her back.'

Henry, very reasonably. But if I hit her back she will hit me again and then we shall have to go on hitting each other all day.

THE OIL LAMPS I bought from the Thieves' Bazaar in Calcutta are a success. My particular thief was a nice-mannered large young man with a shop in a hole by a shed where sheep offal was sold. Now I am glad I braved the Bazaar and the smell and found him; then it was sickening.

The lamps are Victorian and they are beautifully shaped,

gilt, and they give a soft adequate light. People might smile at them, but to me they are far preferable to Aladdins, I would never have a Petrolmax.

We fill them carefully. This I learnt from *The Indian Cook and Housekeeper* by Flora Annie Steel, published in 1888. It is the only book on housekeeping that is any use to me here; I am deeply grateful to Flora Annie Steel and feel she has taken me back fifty years into a former quiet graciousness. She has taught me how to look after my lamps, how to trim them and fill them so that they do not smell. Even lamp-filling can become a ritual.

Now that I have space to think I know how ugly and complicated my domestic life has been and I hope I shall never fall into that ugliness again—on any excuse. I feel I am learning how to live and the key to this part of it is a kind of gravity, complete simplicity, and absence of hurry. These combined have made me like work that I disliked very much before. I am living with a new simplicity and absence of hurry and I have more time than ever before. I shall try and keep like this, always.

Here it is easy. The day, the dailiness of Chinglam, has something of Chinese in it; it is grave and thinking and it is always interesting. I want to learn it, remember it and carry it further; for the children as well as myself; for the children because it is an essential part of living and one that should be learned properly; for myself because I want to enjoy it.

We must have customs—festivals—mark the seasons of the year.

THE LAMPS GIVE a gentle light that make me wonder why I lived so long with electric light. I like to come home from a ride and see the rooms in order and lit with this soft light; I like the windows showing blue squares of twilight outside, and I like the children and pekinese scampering to meet me and the servants coming along the verandah, white shapes in the dusk, and I like the other little white shape of the Munshi's pony that I have hired, going away through the tea.

The house begins to feel like home. But I am wary; I have had so many homes.

I HAVE BOUGHT the Munshi's pony. Everyone is delighted, particularly the Munshi because I have paid too much. I am not sorry, because I like the pony; why be sorry whatever you have spent if you really like what you have bought? He has a gentle nature and a pretty, gentle face and he is big enough and powerful enough to feel like a horse when I ride him.

A pony is a necessity here. All the assistants had pony allowances. Peter is capable of taking me even to Darjeeling.

He is a little gelding but he was called Miss Jim. The children and Giovanna rename him; Giovanna calls him Peter the Rock because she hopes he will be as strong and steady, and the children call him Peter Rabbit. That does not suit him badly; he has the same endearing expression.

With him comes: a small boy to cut his grass, the promise of manure for my canna lily beds, bags of corn to help supply the manure, and a flight of very bold sparrows to steal the corn. The house feels enlarged and I feel we are settled more firmly in.

Tea Dust and Servants.

The head Munshi from Rungolo brought me today the free tea given by the factory every month to all the people on the garden. It occurs to me that I am the only person on the garden who does not get free tea.

There are twenty-two pounds of tea for our house divided into eleven parts. Yes, it is true; I have eleven servants and I cannot help it. I had thirteen, but I sent the cook away and Ears and Giovanna do the cooking. Then I sent the groom away, now the garden-boy and the grass-cutter look after the pony.

The cook was very turbulent and left partly because he was turbulent and partly because he had foot rot, a disease these people get easily in the rains. I was sorry for him, the soles of his feet were cracked to the flesh and he could not walk; I tried to dress them but the smell and his rudeness were too much and with Ears' help I turned him out of the house. Ears' help is not much on these occasions; he is too gentle.

The Calcutta servants have never seen so much tea all at once before; for the first time it is they who are astonished and the garden servants who are blasé. I weigh it out from a great pile on the floor; the house servants do theirs up in newspaper and the outside servants lay cloths down on the floor and make low salaams.

The roll of the servants' pay is interesting from a social point of view. It sounds shameful but, going into statistics with W., it is adequate. Each garden man gets land, a house, house maintenance, free seed, free wood for fuel, medical attention and education for his children, though this last is not compulsory. All the garden-born servants get these advantages. I am only responsible for the servants I bring in.

The servant roll is:—

Ears	Rs 35 /-	monthly
Mrs. Ears	Rs 25/-	"
Sweeper	Rs 25/-	"
Table Boy	Rs 12/-	"
Waterman	Rs 10/-	"
Woodcutter	Rs 9/5/-	"
Bread-runner	Rs 12/-	"
Garden Boy	Rs 8/6/-	"

Washerman	Rs 16/-	"
Caretaker (Baju)	Rs 10/-	"
Grass Cut	Rs 4/4/-	"

Note the difference between the pay of garden men and servants from outside. Lena is paid Rs 50/- and she is the only one who asks me for advances.

The grass-cut is called the 'patta wala', literally 'leaf-man'. He has curious eyes, no muscles in his eyelids so that he cannot lift them; he only sees a line of light. The doctor babu tells me that only a plastic surgeon could help him, and there are no plastic surgeons here. He manages very well; he has a sickle as sharp as a razor, but so far every evening he has managed to bring himself intact back with his two bundles of grass. He is paid two annas a day.

September 1st.

I get up and write in the very early morning when it is fine. It is getting finer. The rains are nearly gone. My desk is put out on the path where the lemon trees almost make an arbour. Out in the blue is really true for Chinglam; it is out—in—up in the blue. At half-past five the light lies unevenly over the valley and on the clouds. The garden is very wet and there is a smell of lemons and roses.

Later the children go up to wash their faces in a spring that flows out from a bamboo pipe in the mountain-side;

the spring is clean and the water from the pipe is cold and strong. When Giovanna was a little girl she used to run up the mountain to wash her face like this, and Giovanna is the sun and the moon and the stars to the children and they follow faithfully in her footsteps.

After they have washed they run down the paths through the tea to breakfast. Giovanna yodels and the sound rings right across the valley. The coolies love it, it is nearly as loud as the gong. Soon they learn to copy it and the valley is filled with yodels.

THE PLUMBING AT Chinglam is charming and effective. Its waterworks go over all the hill; it is a chain of bamboos. Bamboos are hollow and these are split lengthways to make a water channel that is held up on tripods of lesser bamboos. Each of the water-channel bamboos is arranged a little higher than the other so that the water runs down it and falls with a splash to the lower one, and so on and so on, right down the hill from the spring to the house. The air is full of these infinitesimal splashes. In this way the water can go anywhere that is slightly downhill. There is no limit to where it can go and no limit to the bamboos, but there is sometimes a limit to the water because sometimes in the spring, the springs dry up.

Sanitation at Chinglam is simple too. One stream is clean and one is dirty. In the dirty stream, Kokil the sweeper puts what he calls the pisspots under the run of the stream.

After a few moments he rinses them. The pots are clean; the stream runs on.

> Bamboos grow in Japan but they grow in India too and they are trees with one long tall stalk like a feather and they grow lots together, lots in the jungle and lots on the mountain. The coolies use them all day long, they make things with them. Nearly everything. They make houses and cooking pots and benches and they make baskets for their ponies and baskets for theirselves. Our swing is made of bamboos and our chicken run and all our little fences round the flowers they are made of splitted bamboo, and our water comes down the hill in bamboos too.
>
> They are very beautiful and how useful they are and they are green and white inside and there are some other kinds as well.
>
> Rafael. Essay on Bamboos.

September 5th.

In the crevices of the waterfalls we find begonias, small ones, crisp, with heavy leaves; in colour and crispness each petal is like a delicate pink shell. They grow far back under the boulders, under the dripping water, the splash of the little waterfalls themselves. We cannot see through the big falls, they are solid and deafening, as thick and heavy as big icicles. The giant at the head of the valley we have not yet reached.

There is a pool that the children have found in the clean stream that runs through the glade beside the house; it is a pool under the roots of a tree and it is a whole little world in itself. It has depths under the roots where the water seeps away to cavernous gloomy banks horrid with fungus, and it has clear shallow spaces where the pebbles reflect the sun, and the sky is reflected there too, and ferns like trees, and forget-me-nots that seem to be people in summer hats looking at themselves in the water.

This is how Rafael sees it. The children disappear and play there all day long, and Rafael says she makes another pool in her bucket and in it are pebbles and sand and ferns and the sun is reflected there too.

Toys.

When Henry came to stay he brought a box of beautiful and expensive toys; he had a motor-boat that really went and a Meccano and a fire engine with lights and a dog that walked on a lead and a box of plasticine.

Rafael. Oh, I wish I was Henry! Why can't I be like Henry?

Henry, coldly to me. Haven't your children any plasticine? They can't model with mine.

'My children model with clay.'

Henry. Oh! (After a moment.) Where is it?

'It isn't in a box, Henry. You have to go and dig it. Then you mix it with water—'

Henry, with a gleam in his eye. Can I do it?

For a few days Rafael played with plasticine, Henry played with clay, then they both played with clay.

Where are Henry's toys now? They are in the bottom of the cupboard. And where is Henry? He and the other children are playing by the pool. They are having a cigarette tin shop and they are selling leaves and pebbles and bracken-tips and tea flowers, and sand and water lemonade in bottles; they are pledged not to drink the lemonade but they make it just the same; and in the pool are moored three boats, three chips of wood loaded with toadstools and more pebbles and tethered by a piece of cotton tied to a twig.

September 6th.

Chinglam has a history. You can feel this in its brooding peace.

Once it used to be an orchard; it had peach and apple and pear trees and an orange grove and still, in the garden and among the tea, are stumps of fruit trees that belonged to it then. There is a thin old pear and an apple by the swing. The rest were cut down to make room for the tea. Among the tea bushes you come upon an old stump with true apple bark and lichen on it. I wonder if, in the spring, there is ever a twig of blossom?

And on the Saddle there were deodar trees, a fine high row of them, and travellers from Sikkim used to see them from the mountains and then they knew they were in sight of India, of Hindustan. These too were cut down for the tea.

It is difficult to realise the value of tea. How can a single tea garden, for instance, stand the expense of a suspension bridge like the one to Rungjeli that cost sixty thousand rupees? The answer is: easily. Last year W. made four hundred and fifty thousand pounds of tea. This year he will pass half a million. Even a suspension bridge can be paid for from small green leaves like these.

To SHOP AT Chinglam is different from any other shopping. There is a village on the garden and there the Kyah keeps a shop for the coolies and at it we buy kerosene oil, horse-food, matches, potatoes and dhall but not rice. Dhall is a small red native lentil and is usually eaten with rice, but rice is not sold at the Kyah's shop. Why he sells only these few things I do not know. Occasionally he sends word that he has some speciality, like shoe-polish or onions. On Sundays there are small markets in the villages, and Ears goes to our village and buys chickens, and sometimes some bananas and, always, chilis for himself. Giovanna calls these 'pepperonis' and falls on them with delight.

'Be careful, Giovanna. They are far more hot than Italian ones.'

But Giovanna does not believe me and puts one whole in her mouth. When she bites it she screams and spits, but for the rest of the day she cannot get rid of the burning and her eyes are full of tears, streaming down all day.

On Sunday mornings Giovanna goes to the fruit market at Rungli-Rungliot.

Giovanna. I cannot go to Mass. Very well, I go usefully to market instead.

There is no Mass because there is no church. The market is seven miles away, the church is eighteen and Giovanna appears to do quite well without it. She rides Peter and with her she takes Monbad, a basket and perhaps twelve annas.

Monbad rides a pack pony and this is the treat of the week for him. He and Giovanna cannot speak to one another. Giovanna speaks Italian, German, French and English; Monbad speaks Hindustani and Paharia; but they go off together and will come back, about lunch-time, with enough vegetables and fruit to last us for a week. Giovanna tells me she picks them all out with her own fingers; one day I must go and watch the people's faces while she does it.

The market is only a line of sellers who have sat down along the road above the post-office. They each have a mat on which they spread out the things they have for sale. Most of them have come in from outlying villages with pineapples and oranges and lemons and eggs, but there is a professional shopman who sells beads and combs and ribbons and cloth and shirts, and another with secondhand bottles.

It is owing to Giovanna that my store-room is a satisfactory delight. After she has come back on a Sunday it is rich and full of colour. The vegetables are arranged on the shelves against the whitewash, the colours of tomatoes and heads of cabbage and carrots and red-brown onions and thin green beans; there is another sort of bean that is a purplish pink and there is the brilliant hard red of radishes; there are aubergines and the green and cream of leeks and there are rows of oranges and a dish of lemons and a box of Sikkim apples, and a pile of tree tomatoes, globe shapes that are a deep fruit pink. Then there are tins and jars of stores, and a row of home-made jelly and another of marmalade, the first I have ever made. There are crocks of grain: wheat, rice, barley, dhall and atta, and a gallon tin of sugar. There are clean piles of dusters and a medicine-chest and a list of servants' names and wages. Against the wall are bags of gold-coloured Indian corn for Peter and the hens. There is a smell of tea and coffee and medicines and fruit and clean starched linen. It is the core of the house.

Giovanna comes back with another basketful. She has a bunch of carrots and a bunch of marigolds tied to her saddle and Monbad has a yard of sugar-cane of a deep mottled purple. They spill out on the table, beans and carrots, and a marrow and oranges and leeks.

'How much did you spend?'

They spent eight or ten annas. Marrows are two annas and pineapples the same, and bananas are brought to us still in their clusters from the tree and we pay ten annas for about six dozen.

Apart from the market and the Kyah we depend on the bread-runner.

When I arrived at Chinglam, M. handed me a collection of little books with tear-out counterfoils, like chequebooks. There was a book for the baker, the grocer; for everyone. Three times a week I fill in my orders in these books and in the evening the runner comes for them.

He stands by Ears, to whom I give the slips and my instructions; Ears hands them on to the runner speaking in Paharia; the runner receives them one by one and puts them away in his breast pocket, saying over what he has been told; he takes the money and spends it carefully in his mind to make sure he has enough. He salaams and goes to his house which is just behind the cook-house. He is an elderly man, a grandfather, with a fine strong face that has hardly any wrinkles; his hair is white but his skin is a clear deep brown and he stands completely straight. He wears shoes, loose cotton pantaloons, a dark blue serge coat and a muffler round his head. I can trust him with two or three hundred rupees and he does not get muddled with his orders.

In the morning, at four o'clock, he will start on his run to Darjeeling, which is eighteen miles away and three thousand feet up the mountain. He will arrive there about nine o'clock, do all the shopping, have some tea at a teahouse, and start back again at eleven, stopping at the end of the road to have some food before he comes down the hill. He will get back at about four, coming down the hill at an even pace, his basket strapped to his back, some of the weight of it carried by a strap round his forehead, his stick in his hand. The basket is a special one, long-shaped in compartments, and it will hold twenty pounds. He brings bread, butter, vegetables, stores, jams, cheese, cream, dog food, medicines, sewing materials, books, stationery; everything that is needed in the house for two or three days. He goes three times a week, thirty-six miles each time. For this he is paid twelve rupees a month.

September 8th.

A house is like a body; the husband is the head: the children the hands who go out and do things, touch things, contact: and the woman should be the heart. Now I have to be the head and the heart and I should far rather, a thousand times rather, be the hands. I want to touch—to feel—to do—to do so much, and it seems to me now that when I was free I was too ignorant and too blind to see what I could do.

To be tied makes me impatient, terribly uneven; but I am beginning to know the children again. Rafael writes me letters. She addresses the envelope simply: To 'She'.

LENA IS UNHAPPY. She tells me that she only stays because she promised me she would. I say I cannot remember the promise and beg her to go and she says that she only stays because she will not leave me. I point out how perfectly we can manage without her, how Henry does not need her when Giovanna is here, how little Ayah, Mrs Ears, has to do, how pleasant it will be to go back to Calcutta; she says she is very unhappy but will bear it for my sake. She adds that she will send for her husband.

'It was arranged that he should stay in Calcutta.'

Lena. Yes, but I am unhappy. It is better that he should come. Because I am unhappy—because it is cheaper.

She is Christian, once Nepali, married to a Mahommedan. This is an unusual and unsavoury mixture and it stinks. He drinks and beats her and she keeps him on her pay. Even Lena with her stolid fat greedy face has her troubles.

But I do not want her husband here.

SEPTEMBER 10TH.

The walls of this house are so white that on very hot days they take a reflection of green from the garden. It is hot just now when it does not rain. The roof extends in a porch that is covered with fever-creeper that has flowers in groups of tiny heads like primulas, coloured in red and orange and yellow round which the butterflies like to come. The butterflies are fantastic in numbers and size; they are all huge and some are black and crimson, some are black and canary, some are peacock and some are simply brown when they close their wings and purple blue spotted with white when they open them.

It is good to keep a woodcutter instead of buying fuel. The logs come in freshly cut and, if it has been raining, and usually it has been raining, we have to bake them and the sap runs out into the fender.

It is this that gives our evenings such a delicious smell; besides this smell of wood sap there is always a smell of wood-smoke and flowers and the smell of the beeswax polish that I have learnt to make myself.

Now the evenings begin to be familiar. They are proving themselves to be pleasant friendly evenings.

THE MUNSHI FROM whom I bought Peter Rabbit comes to visit me.

Each section of the garden has a Munshi; Chinglam, Rungjeli and Rungolo. The Rungolo Munshi is known as the 'Big Babu' and he is the head under W., but each Munshi is head of his section. Under him are three chaprassi, one for the men coolies, one for women, one for girls and boys and children, though hardly any children work on this garden. For every twenty coolies, under the overseer, there is a foreman called a duffadar and for the work and behaviour of his coolies he is responsible to the overseer who in his turn is responsible to the Munshi. The Munshi is paid perhaps forty-five to sixty rupees a month, but he gets commission and a head price on the number of coolies who turn out to work each day.

Chinglam Munshi is an elderly man like a brown Chinese, plump and strong. He wears white pantaloons, a tweed coat, a round little hat like Ears' and a silver watch. His house has an upstairs and a downstairs, rare on this garden; it is squeezed against a shelf of rock and has a tin roof and a balcony full of flowers. It has also a row of pigeon-houses made of kerosene tins, a stone barn and a stable and an outhouse. The Munshi by garden standards is rich.

He has two surprising things: a son who holds a commission in the Army and a four-hundred-rupee wireless set. The son is a 2nd Lieutenant; the Estate gives one wireless set to each division of the garden for propaganda and the Munshi keeps it in his house and gives out the news.

My encounters with the Munshi have been sudden; Peter stops when he reaches his old stable, nearly throwing us over his ears.

The chickens were bought to eat, but every time we want one Giovanna pleads that it needs more fattening. I did not dream they would become so personal. Their corn is ground down in our own hand mill, and the children work under Giovanna picking special sorts of grass alleged to be good for chicken insides. These chickens now all have Italian names; the hens are Signora Padua, Signora Negra, Biondina, Leoparda; I can never remember them all, but the first two chickens are Angela and Renato, names reserved for Giovanna's own children '*when* they are born, *if* they are born, se piace a Dio!'

I am not popular. The children come around me with suspicious and angry faces when I am ordering the food. 'You are not going to kill Giovanna's *friend*?'

They come and ask me to buy a cock they have seen in the village.

Rafael. A cock like a bride. White as satin!

I say our cock would not like it. They are very cast down. Then I am asked to name two new little chickens, ridiculous white short-winged things with chippy beaks and chippy legs. I say unfeelingly: 'Risotto and Maryland.' Now I am shut out from the chicken world.

September 14th.

We had presents today. Baju brings four papayas for the children. Papayas are a large egg-shaped green fruit with juicy orange-yellow flesh and countless black seeds. You scrape out the seeds, cut the papaya like a melon and eat it with sugar and lemon.

A little boy comes with a very bright beautiful bouquet of zinnias and roses tied with a strip of bamboo bark.

Then M. sends me some violet plants and pineapples, seven in a basket.

After tea I shall plant the violets in the bed under the lemon trees where Baju and I have agreed to plant a violet bed.

Conversation i.

Sabrina. Giovanna, what is this hole in the middle of my tummy?

Giovanna, waggishly. It is not a hole, it is a button.

Sabrina, after a profound contemplation. No: then I think it is a button-hole.

Yesterday a commercial traveller came. He was a little Nepali. It is always an excitement if anybody comes because so few ever come; we can see a stranger a long way off, either down the path from the Saddle or along the road from Rungolo, and when W. and M. come to tea we can put the kettle on at the moment they leave their house and have it boiling by the time they get to ours.

The traveller was travelling in seeds; he was very tired, but I could only buy some snapdragon and verbena and petunia seeds. I like to plant petunia with sweet-peas, the smell of them is heavenly. Among the meanings of 'heavenly' is 'supremely excellent'; that is what sweet- pea and petunia scents are together. I had said I would not care for a garden again, but I am beginning very much to care for this one.

Rafael and Henry are painting vineyards, purple grapes on deep blue paper. Shoomi, Ears' little girl, is sitting on the ground bent forward on her blackboard prostrate with grief. They are at lessons in the arbour of the lemon trees.

'What is the matter with Shoomi?'

Giovanna. She is a very silly girl. You told her to write 'hen' and 'bed' and 'hand', and she writes them all backwards, 'neh' and 'deb' and 'dnah' from right to left. She has no sense.

By desperate efforts and her own zeal, she has attached herself to the children's lessons and learned the English alphabet as far as n. No further. A—n is as far as Shoomi can go, as much as Shoomi's head can hold; to encourage her I find words for her to write that can be contained in a—n.

Shoomi is being petted because she has sat on a bamboo, fallen on it, and the stake of it has gone inches deep into her small slim buttock and every day she has to have it dressed.

It is a hideous wound and though I do not like Shoomi as much as her two younger sisters, I pet her and give her sweets if she does not cry. Her small flat rather sly face has lighted up and she has blossomed into the English alphabet. Now she is rubbing out all her chalked letters with tears and her distracted snub nose.

SEPTEMBER 16TH.

Would you rather have a clean mind in a dirty body or a dirty mind in a clean body? I think I should prefer the clean mind in a dirty body, though I know most people would choose it the other way round.

SEPTEMBER 17TH.

I plant sweet-peas. A coolie comes and makes beautiful tall turrets for them to grow up, lacing the tops into a crown, only he puts them outside the sweet-peas so that they would have grown up in cages. The turrets are too beautiful to touch so we dig up the sweet-peas. I do not know what this will do to them.

In the garden, I can only experiment; I do not know enough to do anything else and there is not even a book on gardening here.

Everywhere, in every bed, there are enormous marigolds blotting out the view, blotting out the beds. Some of them are as tall as I. They have been planted by Baju. I order them to be dug up, one bed at a time. We have no garden-boy as I asked W. to remove him, so that Baju had to dig them up himself. He does it quietly, but at the fifth bed he begins to laugh. It is a dreadful sort of laughing, like weeping. I hear it long after it has stopped, but I have the marigolds dug up all the same.

What else is there in the garden? Wild coffee flowers, roses, Japanese lilies, two dahlias and three big bushes of yellow jasmine; these and the lemon trees. The lemon leaves smell delicious if you crush them in your hand.

Below them, only a few feet down, is a tropical shelf of garden with pineapples and palms and hideous useful bananas.

Rafael. I love bananas. Why *need* they look like that?

Why need they? They grow in a cluster, hanging down below the leaf and from the cluster a dreadful bare wrinkled stalk ends after two or three feet in a bud, a bud with slimy purple folds that looks, for no reason, most obscene. Below the pineapples and bananas is the tea with the paths criss-crossing invitingly through it to the river and the shade trees looking like green bird feathers in the darker bushes.

From the village, where most of the Chinglam labour lives, sounds come faintly up to us in the evening. There are no sounds in the day-time because the men and women and some of the children have gone working; even the babies are gone in basket cradles on their mothers' backs. Beyond the village is the leaf shed where the leaf is weighed and in the evening the pluckers run down the hill laughing. The sound comes up to our garden in bright-edged little waves. I am beginning to distinguish the faces now. I know some of the coolies and they know me. They smile and salaam.

The coolie who makes the turrets is more good-looking than any coolie I have seen. He has lustrous dark-fringed eyes and a skin coloured yellow ivory. After he finishes his

work he does not go away but stays watching us, particularly the children, particularly Sabrina.

Two hens have laid eggs, Gioello del Cuoco and Signora Padua. This, to us, is a miraculous birth. I do not know if it is Giovanna's feeding, but the shells are a deep clear brown pink, not at all like other hens' eggs here.

Some local hen-keepers come to see. Giovanna is very proud and Ears hopefully marks the eggs, 1 and 2.

September 18th.

The beautiful coolie came again today. I ask him if he would like to be the garden-boy. He says he would and I send him to W. He comes back and says he is engaged; he will help Baju with the garden, look after Peter and run errands and go up seven miles to the post. For this he will be paid Rs 9/- a month.

When I had told him this, he made a long impassioned speech in Paharia to Ears. I thought he was saying, very rightly, that the work was much and the pay too little.

I begin to say that I agree when I am hastily hushed by Ears. The boy was saying: 'Tell the lady she must not be angry if I make mistakes because I shall make mistakes. I am only a country boy and if she gets angry I shall get frightened and then how shall I do my work?'

September 19th.

He does make mistakes. When he harnesses Peter I find the bridle straps over his nose and in front of his ears, but no one could be angry with the garden-boy; he gives a flashing deprecatory smile and his lashes that are long and dark and silky fall and rise with his anxiety and a flow of Paharia that I cannot understand comes out in explanation.

In the very early morning from our first day I am woken by my own cock. I have never had one before and it wakes only me; the children and Giovanna sleep through its crowing.

I lie and think about the day. Today, I shall plant more violets, I shall work, I shall walk up on the Ridge and I shall finish reading *The Snow Queen* to the children. In Chinglam, most of what I plan comes true and that has seldom happened to me in any other place. The days were stolen before they had begun; I think I never saw a day. When I was a child I remember days that stretched into infinity with the certainty of other infinite days; certain, unhurried and brimmingly full.

Now a little of that length seems coming back to me; the days are quieter, longer, more sure, than any since my childhood; their uneventfulness makes them full because all the small things, things that I have not had time to notice, have space to come to life as they did then; but it is a development from then, more definite, more wonderful because it is backed with full-grown powers and a grown-up's knowledge; I get a double delight from the things that delighted me then, that delight Rafael now. She sees the gulf from the Saddle exactly as it is, sharply and minutely, every curl in the clouds, every colour on the Leopard's Scar, the shadow of each falcon's wing; I can see it as she does, but it brings me echoes and allusions as well: of books, of pictures, of experience, and it starts thoughts in my mind.

There should be time for life like this. I have moments of feeling alive that I have not known for years. I hardly recognise myself; it is bliss.

I plan my day and the day comes to pass. I have expectations of violets, work, the opening of the clouds before the snows that I can see from the Ridge, and in the evening *The Snow Queen*.

The cock crows and I get up.

'LIFE IS PASSING over my head,' sighs Giovanna.

'Yes. Now why won't you be a sensible girl and leave me for that good post in —?'

Giovanna has eyes very bright and eloquent and friendly, of the colour that goes with woods and streams; they are the colour brown of the stones in the water and have flecks of green in them like infinitesimal leaves. Now they are brighter with tears.

'I do not want to go,' says Giovanna. 'I feel me here to be in Switzerland. I am not homesick, I am not discontent. I don't know why. It is much better here than to be in a town. I am for the mountains and the natural … and my chickens … and the garden with the salads that will soon be ready … I have planted the salads … and for the children … Now, after so long, they have affection …'

But all the same I know she will have to go. Apart from anything else, she is only twenty-six; it is too lonely here for her.

September 20th.

Each house here is a homestead. There is one below Chinglam and it is as complete as an island is complete. I learn it as I should learn a lesson. I want to know these people.

It is built on a small hill cleared out of the forest and on the flanks of this hill are the owners' fields, now planted with millet; they rise to touch the buildings themselves. The buildings are round a courtyard of pale baked earth, the house at one end, the out-houses the other, and the two side walls are lined with kerosene tins raised on stilts for chickens. Also raised is a stook of Indian corn, on a tripod of bamboos; the husks are withered dark brown, and to the top poles of the tripod someone has tied bunches of marigolds. There is a pumpkin patch and pumpkins ripening on the house roof; green chillies are spread there as well; the red ones hang on strings under the eaves. The roof is thatched, and so are the roofs of the out-houses.

There is an orange grove and some white goats; there are banana trees and pineapple bushes with a thatched platform in the middle of them on which the family take turns to sit, to scare away civet cats now that the pineapples are ripening. There is a poinsettia hedge and marigolds and roses. There is a huge old shiny log that the men use as a sawing-block and there are a great many baskets: carrying cone-shaped baskets in all sorts of sizes to fit all sorts of backs, flat sifting baskets, small containing baskets standing on small feet, and pack-pony panniers.

I know exactly what the inside of the house is like. Its walls are of thick baked earth leeped in a pink-brown plaster wash that is renewed before the Durga pujah every year. There is only one room and it has a shelf made of built-up earth leeped to the wall and on it are a row of brass platters and goblets; platters and goblets are plates and cups. Perhaps there is a piece of mirror, perhaps even a whole mirror painted with flowers, and there are pictures cut from illustrated papers pasted on the wall. All the family possessions are kept in wooden chests or bazaar tin boxes along the wall and the sleeping mats and quilts are rolled up against them. There might be a small wooden pillow, there will be a hand-grinding mill, and a fire between the holes of a small earth oven built on the floor with an iron or copper pot cooking over it and earthenware water pots beside it.

If there is a baby it will have a basket slung outside on the verandah from the roof like the lost boy's cradle in Peter Pan.

Outside the house, from tree to tree in the orange grove, fly two black and white magpie-robins; they are very like magpies and not at all like robins, except for the way they turn their necks and a look in their eye.

GAMES AFTER TEA.

'What is this card, Rafael?'

Rafael. The two of digs.

'Let us play Animal, Vegetable and Mineral. You know that game, but do you remember what a mineral is? A mineral is a metal. You are sure you understand?'

Rafael. Yes.

Henry. Yes.

Henry, after a minute. Did you say 'metal' or 'nettle'?

YESTERDAY WE PLANTED the petunia and snapdragon seeds in seed boxes. M. sent me cornflowers and from Calcutta I had a present of Chinese forget-me-nots. Baju likes working with flowers. He cut the wooden seed boxes in half and divided them into compartments made symmetrical with bamboo.

W. comes riding up the zigzags from the river. All the

lessons stop, the children run out to clasp his legs and Ears breaks into a smile and goes to cool beer in the stream. Baju comes round, poking with a small stick among the flowers, he is giving for W. an imitation of a busy chowkidar busily working.

W. tells me that when the last manager died here after twenty-six despotic years' rule of the garden, Baju went to the funeral. The assistant then at Chinglam offered to drive him in his car but the old man would not presume to get into it and chose to run behind it all the way. He took a bunch of violets to put on the coffin and did the real deep prostration salaam before it. W. says that the manager's personal bearer, to whom he had shown great kindness, was sitting outside smoking a cigar when the coffin was carried downstairs.

Baju is the old good type, but like so many of the old good type, he drinks too much. He is nearly always a little drunk and sometimes he is far too drunk and then he is noisy and tiresome and erratic.

I think he is matched by the clock in my office. It is almost as old, with a loud rusty tick and it strikes the half hours at the hours and the hours at the half. It is just about as confused as he.

I STILL GET up to work at half-past five and after the first wrench it is worth it; only it is so lovely that I look at the valley and forget to work. It is warm and fresh and the sun is only beginning and strikes across the valley and arrives low on the ground, on the undersides of bushes and below the coffee flowers, so that they are gold underneath and rimmed with gold as if they had haloes.

Reading Gorman's Life of Joyce, I am oppressed again by the robustness of these men. I never long to be a man as much as in my writing; to be a man, because I should have a man's wholeness. To me that is what a woman can never be; I think she can never be whole, whole physically or whole hearted. If she is whole then she is useless as a woman. She must be continually impaired; by marriage, by children, by duties and ties; drained, as she is drained by her menses each month. Complete wholeness is male, a woman cannot hope to achieve it and the lack of it shows in her work. To the extent that she is masculine she approaches it, to the extent that a man is feminine he loses it, but men have this robust easy power and they do not even know they have it; it is an unconscious lordliness. It is no use resenting it. I do not resent it. I can only recognise it and do what is within my power. Anything else would be hideous.

Caste.

Ears and his family are Lepchas, an old gentle race that is dying because its people have been overlaid by the more robust, more ordinary Nepali. Ears is a typical Lepcha and it is this that makes him of little help as a head man in the house; he cannot order the lesser servants, he can only ask them and chuckles gently if they are difficult. The waterman is very large and unruly; he looks a cross between a hunter and the tiger he might be hunting; he swings tins of water and billets of wood as if they weighed nothing and strides magnificently between the cookhouse and the bathrooms. I can tell by the way Ears laughs with him on the verandah that he is afraid of him.

The table boy, Monbad, is a Chetri, next to Brahmin. He has a pale refined face and beautiful manners. Ears and the water-man are high enough for him to consort with, though what religion Ears has is Buddhist.

Lena is a Kami, very low caste, almost an untouchable, and she has turned Christian. The other servants despise her, but they come to me in pity.

Ears. Memsahib, Lena Ayah has a lot of trouble. Let her husband come.

'You would like him to come? I will let him come if you like.' I watch them and say slowly, 'His name is Huq.'

A tremendous change of expression, incredulous and shocked.

'Yes. He is a Mohammedan. Lena married him.'

Silence.

'Would you still like him to come?'

Monbad. I should have to leave, or I could not go into my village.

Ears. No one would visit us.

Lena's husband does not come.

SEPTEMBER 21ST.

Today we see the Sikkim snows without clouds from the Saddle. They seem small, almost like sugar lumps over distant ranges; those ranges are blue, the closer ones green and the green ones look huge to us because they are so close, with firs and spruce going up to the skyline and the Leopard's Scar going down on the right. This is a landslide where there are particularly many leopards. It is these green mountains towering over us that cut off our sun at four o'clock.

As we stand there, on the narrow ridge rising up into the sky, the path leads away to where the wild cherry trees go up to the Viewpoint opposite Kanchenjunga. Behind us, spread along the valley, is our own Chinglam tea. Already we are possessive about it. The children say, 'Our tea tastes far the best.' It is very good quality tea.

THE MAGNOLIA-COLOURED PEKINESE, Comfort, produced three puppies, quickly and tempestuously with only a little help from me. They are dark-coloured at present, with primrose linings to their tails and a pale sheen on their darkness if you hold them up to the light that shows they will be gold.

They are as big as mice, but have heads as blunt and smooth as a seal's; they are in fact a mixture between a mouse and a seal reduced down one thousand times.

I go in and tell the children the puppies are born. They are supposed to be informed with all the facts, but Henry is vague.

Henry, turning up his face to me. Is their mother born too?

September 25th.

All afternoon I bed out forget-me-nots and plant mignonette in supreme serene peace. The feeling of the earth and the tiny pale plants and the sun on my back under my hat is soothing.

The hats we wear here are sold in the streets in Calcutta for eight annas; they are huge and made of yellow country straw; they make Giovanna look Mexican. We have Kashmiri shoes, an inside sock of goatskin laced up the front and a heavier leather sandals with wide cross-overs and nails. They are wonderfully comfortable. The children look like infant hunters in theirs.

When I have finished I call Giovanna to admire the vision I see of a spread of forget-me-nots underneath the roses.

Rafael calls me when she is lying down. She is lying on her back with her knees on the pillow and a hiatus between her vest and her knickers showing a moon of stomach. Her clothes hang on the bedpost and her hair is turned up in plaits with ribbons and her eyes are turned up too, looking at the ceiling.

Rafael. Fetch your typewriter. I have thought of some poems and I want you to put them down.

I put them down as she tells me:

1. Cockadoodle do,
   The morning is not through,
   Every time you eat your food
   You must say your prayers.

2. White cock, coloured cock,
   Where have you been all the summer?
   We have been sailing the sea
   Across the dancing sea.

3. Rose, Rose,
   I pick you often
   And put you into a vase;
   But when you die of life
   I throw you into the bucket.

Rafael. Aged 5.

The woodcutter and the son of the bread-runner have gone to the war. The thought of the woodcutter fills me with trepidation; he is a wild uncouth halfwitted creature who has no idea of what he does. I think they have taken him because he is a fine specimen physically.

He is less than half-civilised. To see him coming out of the forest when he has cut his load of wood, bare-legged, bare-footed, wild-haired, with a naked kukri knife is terrifying.

He will have to wear boots, learn Urdu; he has never earned more than nine rupees a month, but now he will get eighteen rupees for pocket money, not to live on, but to spend; every necessity will be given him and some of them are necessities it has never occurred to him to need.

I went to sympathise with the bread-runner, but he was not at all sad, he was elated; every recruit gets an advance to give to his relatives, and that had healed grief.

This makes thirty-five men gone off this division of the garden.

September 28th.

After the rains the hills have a peculiarly sparkling blue air with a feeling of snow in it. There is the beginning of the feeling of holiday too. In every village the pampas grass is as high as the new prayer flags put up on the Ridge; it is the sign of the autumn and the pujas that are coming.

The huts are thick with marigolds and zinnias and roses and yellow daisies. Pumpkins lie in their vines on the roof, ripening in the sun, and now, usually, there is sun; the clouds stay down in the bottom of the valley in long Chinese shapes.

THIS MORNING THE servants found the pug marks of a leopard on the flower beds near the chicken house. It had walked in and out of my turrets of sweet-peas. I expect it was on its way from this range to the next.

There came a curdling scream from Giovanna. How we ran to her. It was a butterfly that had settled on her shoulder. It was black with shimmering blue swallow tails at least six inches across. The scream had frightened even it and it had gone.

'Why did you scream? You were not afraid of a butterfly.'

Giovanna. No, not at all, but, madonna santa, I always have to scream. Even when I most don't want, still I have to scream.

AS EVERY STATE in Europe used to have its Jew, so every tea garden has to have its Kyah.

All through the gardens there is a chain of shops, all the same, poor and open-fronted, with matting on the floor, a pair of scales and shelves round its three walls; on the shelves are baskets of atta flour and dhall and onions and ginger roots, packets of matches, tins of kerosene, cheap sweets loose in jars and bolts of cloth that are either prints with a design of white on green, blue, purple or magenta, or else coolie velvet that is made with a short nap-like plush in beautiful jewel shades. All over the roof hang head-shawls embroidered and plain; they are made of brilliant wool and have the bird colours I see on the women, parrot-green and blue and yellow, but some are a clear orange the exact colour of the puja marigolds. In the middle of the floor, the Kyah sits cross-legged and his cash desk, a few inches high, is close by him.

He sells the things in his shop and anything else that may be required. He used to lend money, but the Moneylenders Act has spoilt his power there; at one time he would have half the garden in his hand; coolies, foremen, Munshis, probably the assistants, possibly the manager. Now the companies lend and advance money themselves and the Kyah is limited to cashing cheques; from our small shop the Kyah cashes about six thousand rupees each week.

He is a small oily man with an oily alert and slightly insolent manner and a large nose with sensitive nostrils and large dark eyes. It is easy to see he despises the people here; his prominent features stand out among the flatness of theirs and he is utterly alien. His women are finer and more lovely than the women here and wear more shapely clothes, thin beautifully draped saris. They have appealing and sagacious children with the same dark liquid eyes; they are far more clever than the native children, but always a little slippery and sly; they suffer in school from incessant bullying, but they suffer it in silence.

Men and boys wear distinctive diamond-sided black caps, and when I see one of these shapes coming towards Chinglam above the tea, I know it has come about money.

In the shops, high up under the ceiling, the Kyahs put an altar fringed with lace and garlanded with marigolds; their own small particular God is on it. They have their own ceremonial days and customs and an undercurrent of communication with each other. More and more they remind me of Jews.

I BOUGHT SIX balls of khaki wool to make two army scarves. I have been knitting and knitting and knitting for three months and still I have not finished the first. What slow cramping painful shame.

Lena. I will knit the soldier scarf for you, madam.

In three days it is finished. Mine is still not done.

THE PACK-PONIES HAVE various styles of dress, and all the styles have a meaning; if they are wearing simply a sacking pad with bamboo ropes they are going to fetch luggage; if a pair of wooden prongs, a prong a side, they are fetching wood; if it is a pair of close-woven panniers they are carrying leaf tea, and if these are wide-meshed they are carrying something larger, coal or chickens or stones. Sometimes we meet them on the road to the station and then they are wearing a pair of tea boxes.

The ponies can carry a large weight as long as the balance is kept between the sides, as long as the two sides balance. They are skeleton thin and covered in dirt and sores. They are all cow-hocked, their legs almost meeting behind, and that gives them a cowed look, a whipped-dog look.

On Sundays they have the day off. They wander free; they have not the spirit or the strength to wander far. They crop over the stubble of the fields and along the paths, and they lie down and roll in the dust and sun and scratch their hides against a pray-flag pole.

THE SADDLE IS getting to be my quarterdeck; it is where I go to think and pace and if I have been depressed it seems to rescue me and start me off again.

There is nothing, no one to interrupt. Who could there be? Only I am there and the wind and the clouds and the snows.

I have never felt anywhere more than here the feeling of life flowing that I get at a height; a flowing of it into me and from me into it. I have felt it in Scotland and in Cornwall and in the mountains in Wales, but it is greater here. Today I felt it even more; almost as if I feel what I see, I am what I see.

I sit on a rock and watch the clouds, and I am immeasurably higher than they. I am like Dorothy Wordsworth, 'my heart dissolves in what I see'.

Coming down it is cold. The bamboos are blowing in the wind and the sun is gone. The holidays are coming nearer. As I come down the hill, a drum is beating in the village and, as always now, there is a thread of sound from a flute.

Conversation 2.

Rafael and Henry are talking.

Rafael. I can't marry you, Henry, because I promised Giles, but never mind, Henry, you can be my baby's father.

That will suit Henry. If ever he is asked what he will be when he grows up, he says, 'I want to be a father.'

Happiness when you are miserable.

To plant Japanese poppies with cornflowers and mignonette, and bed out the petunias among the sweet-peas so that they shall perfume each other. To see the sweet-peas coming up.

To drink very good tea out of a thin Worcester cup of a colour between apricot and pink shell.

To have Rafael paint a truly good picture.

To have letters from England and America.

To come into my bedroom and see it orderly and quiet; white walls, wood floor waxed, white rugs and white curtains barred with blue, and the deep-coloured Sikkim blankets turned down on my bed and zinnias in the wall vase, and a little quiet white-dressed ayah with a sweet quiet face waiting to rub my feet.

All these have happened to me today.

Comfort likes to hold a puppy in the crook of her front paw. The expression on her face is as near a madonna as a very Chinese-faced pekinese can get.

The servants come and ask for dearth allowance. This is because of the high price of rice during the war. The allowance, fixed by W. on behalf of the company, is two pice a day, about thirteen pence a month. This is a tremendous advantage; the bread-runner, garden-boy, Baju, the grass-cutter and the wood-cutter will get it.

The company also give an advance for the Puja holidays and I must give it too. It is from two to five rupees and on this there will be magnificent doings. But I have stipulated that my servants take it in turns to get drunk, not do it all together.

I come back late and walk up through the hollow; it is still and green. The stream runs over the stones quietly, as water does run at twilight. There are pampas grasses growing high, the heads of them half against the shade trees and half against the sky, and in the sky is already a star and a new, a crescent moon. The pampas shines and the moon shines, but with a different light; the pampas has a grey plumaged silver shine like the gloss on a bird's wing and the little moon shines young and limpid in the sky. The leaves of the shade trees are like feathers too.

I SPEAK TO Lena about her clothes. I do not like her coming in silks, hennaed and bejewelled to work.

'Lena, have you no white clothes to wear when you are looking after Henry? I like my ayahs to wear white.'

Lena. No Madams I ever worked for requiring uniform, Madam. Moreover, they have given to me saris worth hundreds of rupees.

'You are a Nepali. You shouldn't wear a sari.'

Lena. Sari is universal dress, Madam.

Mrs. Ears gives a sniff. A gentle sniff from Mrs. Ears would be a wound from anyone else.

IT IS THE eve of the Durga Puja and on the roads W. has put up swings for the coolies and all up and down the valley are groups of people swinging.

There will be no more work until the Lakshmi Puja is

ended. The people have their new puja clothes: skirts that swing in pleated folds, blouses of silk and velvet and print, a shawl wound wide round them to bind their waists and breasts, a head veil and heavy jewellery, of brass and country silver and turquoise and a red stone like a berry and whole rupees threaded into leafed necklaces.

One woman has on a blue skirt, green bodice, red waist shawl, brilliant pink head veil; she looks like a kingfisher in the distance. Going along the paths to the swings, the women do look like flocks of brilliant birds: kingfishers, parakeets, minivets, all chattering. Further away still they look like beads or hundreds-and-thousands, those tiny parti-coloured sweets, scattered on the hill.

WE MEET TIBETAN herdsmen driving in goats and sheep to Darjeeling for the holiday feasts.

Rafael is full of pity. The children are acquainted with death because Giovanna has a peasant acceptance of life, and life naturally includes death. The children have the same attitude towards it. It is the only attitude to have. But these sheep are to be eaten and that seems to Rafael a terrible thing and, as we stand in the road, they turn their mild faces to us, staring at the phenomenon of us with no idea where they are going.

'They have had a good life,' I say to Rafael.

All the year they have been grazing on the Tibetan

uplands and they are fat and fat-tailed, and the goats have hair and beards that sweep the ground, hair in smoky colours of grey and white streaks.

The men are not nearly as well dressed as the goats; their overgowns are patched in colours of dirty mustard and blue and grey, and their sleeves are filthy, but not as filthy as their hair that is matted to ropes of dust and filth. Some have prayer wheels of copper and silver to turn in their hands as they follow the flocks; the others laugh and leap about and stare and beat the sheep with staves. The rams turn on them, magnificent rams with angry yellow eyes.

The men are magnificent too, with clear brown skins through which the red shows in their lips and cheeks, they look astonishingly lusty, and all, under their coloured tatters and rags, wear neat Bata sandshoes.

THE CHILDREN ARE envious of the swings. They have a swing of their own, but it cannot compare with these. They are simple, a loop of rope hung from a tripod of bamboos, but men and women swing in them and far out, over the gulf below the road.

In one place further along, there is a kind of a merry-go-round, but it is what they call an over-and-over, four wooden boxes that move over and over on a wooden wheel. This is the high spot of the holidays and literally hundreds will ride on it before the Pujas are finished.

OCTOBER 2ND.

There is holiday in the air. The flute has been going in procession from village to village all day. Its sound is minor, a little melancholy, but exciting.

The villages look very lovely. The millet is high and intensely vividly green, and now the heads of grain are turning bronze and gold. Everywhere among the huts are marigolds, high and spreading, and yellow daisies. There is yellow wherever you look, because these daisies grow wild in quantities in the fields. The moon-flowers are out, great green-white trumpets of flowers hanging down, and there are thousands of cosmos flowers in crude pink and magenta and crimson and white, shaped like narrow-leafed stars.

The sound of the flute comes nearer. A procession is coming down the hill.

I GO TO Darjeeling to see the Puja clothes. They are bright and various.

The Nepali women have cloth gathered into a skirt by pleating the folds in front and twisting them into a knot. They have jackets or blouses of velvet or print and head shawls of plaid and muslin or embroidered wool or coarse hand-made lace. They have necklaces and bracelets and nose rings that catch the light as they move.

There is nothing half as naive about the dresses of the

Sikkimese and Bhutias and Tibetans. Their robes are dark, sternly cut and sweeping in silks with a ground pattern of their own colour that gives a damask effect; the linings are brilliant, showing at the edges or as the wearers move. The sleeves are turned back with a colour of aster pink or Chinese heavenly blue or green the colour of corn. They have a sash of silk and the jewellery is heavy and chased, plaques and pendants on chains, ear-rings and rings. If a woman is married she wears a striped apron with embroidered comers. Her plait may hang down her back or be twisted round her head in a coronet. The clothes are the same for children, but hats are worn only by the men, round Chinese skull caps with a cornelian or coral centre button, fur-lined hats with ear flaps, or a homburg, turned down all the way round with a peacock feather in it. There are boots for the winter made of padded felt worked in patchwork, and sets of bags for money or spices made of patchwork too. Rafael has a set like these.

At night I walk up to Point Clear to look down on the town; there are hundreds of lights under the clouds, and the clouds are white on a cornflower-blue night. Coming down, the rickshaws run by me with a low padding of feet and groans from their runners. In the bazaar, from every house comes music, low exciting music and the air is full of small tinkling temple bells. In the Market there are wild crude Paharia colours and wild crude hill faces, all smiling good-temperedly and most of them a little drunk.

October 4th.

Henry's chicken, Risotto, died in agony after eating a hairy caterpillar.

Giovanna. Because he had no mother to look out for him. Just the same as I.

I have to keep hopping out of the office to save the garden when the garden-boy and Giovanna are working on it; especially Giovanna. She has a passion for tidiness which is not possible or desirable in my jungle garden, and she has a rake, un grande ratello, and she began by raking up all the portulucca that has spread itself into a carpet under the roses exactly as it had said it would in the seed catalogue.

Giovanna. Ah! che zocchola! What a wooden shoe I am!

Nothing else in the garden has behaved at all as the catalogues said. Cornflowers, innumerable cornflowers have come up everywhere; the poppies not at all, and snapdragons in clumps, though they must have crawled about under the earth to do this as they were all carefully and symmetrically sown.

Even after we bedded the cornflowers out, more cornflowers came up.

My forget-me-nots grew and waxed strong and then a suspicion filled me. There was something horribly familiar in their shapes. In a few more days, there was no mistaking it; they were cornflowers.

On the same day Giovanna tore up all the Mexican salvias

that I admit were dying, but dying exquisitely on the fringe of the lawn, turning from purple to mauve to silver, like a row of tassels tossing in the green.

Everything is pervaded by the holidays. I have had to do all my shopping for six days, make all my household arrangements; the bread-runner will not go up to Darjeeling, the wood-cutter will not cut wood and the grass-cutter will only cut grass every other day; all of the servants will be given leave in turn, except Ears and Ayah, who are Buddhist, and Lena who is Christian. I see their houses are decorated all the same.

The first puja is the Durga Puja of the Goddess Durga, the consort of Shiva. She keeps house for him, but once a year she goes back to her father's house; the festival celebrates her visit and in her wake, all the sons and daughters of Hindu Bengal go back to their homes. Durga ends her visit on the fourth day and her spirit is returned to her husband by the immersion of her image in the river; the sadness of her leaving is healed in the puja of her daughter Lakshmi, the Goddess of good fortune, on the day and night of the full moon.

The pujas are more pleasing and naive here than anywhere else I have seen them. The houses are leeped with a fresh red earth wash, the best brass utensils are put out on the shelf and patterns are painted in Indian red and white on the wall behind them and along the verandahs.

Bunches of marigolds and flowers hang head downwards from the ceiling. A few houses have pots of geranium, a few have jasmine, and nearly all have pumpkins ripening on the roof. You do not see how dirty the houses are, they all smell freshly of flowers and the darkness inside them is brightened by the marigolds. Like the people, the houses look inviting now.

THE THREE PUPPIES have been given milk names as all Chinese children should be given; they are called Honey, Bunny and Sunny. They are opening their eyes and their eyes are blue. Do all young babies have blue eyes? Even Chinese ones?

W. IS AT home to his coolies with sports on the football ground. From breakfast-time processions from every village have been streaming towards it. I take Peter, a string of pack-ponies, Giovanna, the children, the servants, the servants' children, and go out to join them.

In the middle of the ground is a guy, a funny man of straw, made to look as much like W. as possible. This is great wit.

At the end of the ground are roped-off boxes; the middle one is for W. and M. and their guests, the left one is for the Munshis' wives and the Kyah's ladies, and the right-hand one is for the prizes.

The prizes, and Henry, Rafael and Sabrina divide equal

attention. The prizes are handsome, blankets, quilts, jerseys, head-shawls, lengths of cloth and mufflers.

The side of the mountain above the ground is a kaleidoscope of colours, shifting, turning, altering, with colours of poppies and marigolds and flax-flowers, and parrot and canary wings, and cherry lollipops.

W. says the sports must not change from year to year. There must be a sack race and searching for pennies in a tub of sawdust with hands tied behind backs; there must be tilting the rings on ponies; these are the pack-ponies who, in spite of sores and thinness, get up a tremendous excitement and dash about ready to tilt at anything; there must be an eating race, when the old men have to eat in the shortest time a pile of parched rice, which is as dry as it sounds, and green bananas which are tough. Sabrina could not get over this.

Sabrina. You see, Giovanna, grown-up people do eat with both hands!

There has to be an egg-and-spoon race, a giggling race, for the unmarried girls, and a dignified musical chairs to the gramophone for the Kyah's ladies. For the rest of us, the band plays: a Tibetan horn, cymbals, our flute, and a great many drums.

The schools have to give a display and Rungjeli school wins with a maypole dance to a solemn chant of 'For he's a jolly good fellow'. If any of the boys go out of step the schoolmaster leaps forward and slaps their ears. There also has to be very tough and bloody wrestling.

In between races the local dancing man goes round; he does not dance, he shuffles in a pair of tennis shoes and twirls a stick and exchanges banter with the people as he passes. A very old man follows him playing bagpipes. It seems tedious to me, but the people laugh every time he moves.

Sweets are distributed, and sugar cane. W. gives away the prizes. I have presented some for the people of Chinglam and get cheered.

W. You are the Princess of Chinglam.

October 8th.

Today the clouds are high and the shadows of them are blown across the hill. I walk on the Saddle. Sometimes I feel my eyes must get big with seeing so far.

The children have made hobby horses of the pampas canes. These have slim stems and their great feathery heads make excellent tails. Some are white, others are green bronze. They go galloping on them down the grass lanes that the paths make between the tea.

Pampas horses are naturally called Pampero, after our friend Bob Skene, the international polo player's, famous favourite horse. Pampero is in America. Bob is in Singapore.

The bagpipes are playing in the village on one side of me, and Giovanna is practising her mandoline on the other. The drums beat late into the night. If you listen to them long enough they seem to be beating inside you. I can understand now why they are so exciting.

The attraction of looking out of the drawing-room windows at dusk is looking into the tops of the trees and the sky and the clouds. Everything is blue, trees, sky, the whole window, only the clouds remain snow white. In the moonlight they grow whiter and whiter, and then the white roses along the path and the pale bamboo poles of the swing catch the light and shine.

There is one particular star that we see at Chinglam, over the chincona mountain; at dusk it is high in the dome of the sky and, as the valley darkens, it comes down in the west and seems to grow larger and larger until the moment when it goes behind the mountain. Then it is enormous and it leaves the sky refulgent.

Conversation 3.

Rafael. I am ill. I have a sore throat at the back of my neck, that's why.

'But you are better. You could trot Peter up and down a little.'

Rafael, indignantly. Of course I can't. I'm far too weak.

NOT ENOUGH HAS been said about Kokil; Kokil is the sweeper, the untouchable, the carrier of night soil, the cleaner of the pots, and he has become in the years we have been together a very real friend. It is difficult to know how this has happened, as we have hardly ever exchanged a word that is not about the dogs or Jeyes Fluid or Bromo. Once, when his little son had typhoid and I sent glucose and Jaffa oranges, he broke into speech and told me about his own land and home. Once a year he takes two months' leave and goes home and begets another son.

He looks as if he would breed sons. He is a tall well-made man looking like a Rajput, the fighting race; he is strong and impressive with big features and a big moustache, more like a general than a sweeper. He wears good clothes, a spotless flowing dhotie, a khaki shirt and a black silk hat, and he has manners and courtesy. His demon is litigation and all his money goes in that.

Here, at Chinglam, he has made himself into a guard for me. If I work late I let the servants go, but Kokil will not go. He waits until I go to bed, sitting on the cold verandah with a lantern and a stick, and however much I order him, he will not go away. Once I came out suddenly and he was reading; he stood up as I came and had to leave his book open on the floor; it was a textbook in English. None of the other servants can even read Urdu.

On feast days Kokil gives the dogs a huge chupatti like a waffle that he buys in the bazaar. Every dog he has looked after, every puppy, remembers and adores him.

THE NAMES OF the central great peaks of the Himalayan snows are Kang Peak, Jannu, Little Kabru, Kabru, Kanchenjunga, Pandim, Simvo, Narsing and Siniolchu. Giovanna first discovered that we could see them from the Viewpoint when Peter ran away with her along the upper path. Even in her fright she was lost in wonder at them.

I SUPPOSE CHILDREN are intended partly as a discipline. Certainly mine are often that to me. It is compulsory stimulation, compulsory taking an interest in what does not interest you. They say it broadens you; but there is a danger of being made so broad that you end quite flat.

Today I have had to talk; intimately about the habits of babies, about Sabrina's table manners, if it is true that guinea pigs do not have tails, whether it is, or is not, necessary for jerseys to be worn, and endlessly about the royal family.

Rafael once went to a fancy-dress party as the Queen of Hearts. That began it. She wears her dress now whenever she can and firmly believes she is as beautiful as Balkis. She is called Queen Purple and Henry is a prince, named simply and suitably, Royal.

All this goes on as firmly and as actively as bees going about their work. I could not stop it, I could only make it

I SHALL ALWAYS feel doubtful about lipstick after living in a betel-nut country. The betel-chewers have red vivid lips; it gives the men a girlish perverted look, until they open their mouths and show their teeth, stained scarlet too. Then they look more than depraved; like Draculas, bloody in every sense of the word.

THE HOLIDAYS ARE over. There is no sign of them today. The gong rang out again and again not a minute before half-past four. The regular end of work time on the garden is five, but Chinglam rings at half-past four; this is because the leaf, if it did not leave the shed half an hour earlier, would make the factory late. It is carried over on pack-ponies; the leaf from Rungjeli comes down a ropeway.

They are plucking on Chinglam today. I watch them from the Saddle. There is no sign of the holidays except sometimes a clean new head-shawl that someone is extravagantly wearing for work, and a marigold garland thrown away on the path. There is also a strong smell of drink about some of the servants. I have not seen Baju for three days.

October 15th.

I walk up on the Saddle and today in strong sunlight it is better than ever. The Sikkim snows are not white but hyacinth blue, the houses of Kalimpong below the Rinchinpong ridge are, every one, clear. They want me to go and live there and I have moods when I want this too; but these are ripples on my contentment. It is hard to be even. I remember when I was studying the lives of nuns for *Black Narcissus* how, in every Order, the virtue of evenness was stressed and how they tried to instil it into the characters of the novices. I do not achieve even the fringe of it.

It is stupid, and a waste of time to be melancholy. I do not want people. I have books, work, a garden; I have the children and the dogs and, when I feel I am getting infantile, I have the books again. I must not count Giovanna. Very soon she is going away, and it is right that she should go.

We go to see the factory. It is a modern, almost suburban building, flat-topped with rows of windows and balconies. Giovanna says it reminds her of a sanatorium in Sierro.

We see the pluckers come in, children and boys and girls and women and men. Men—*marde*—are paid five annas a day; women—*aurats*—four annas; *chokras*—boys and girls—two annas; and *lokras*—children—one anna. If a coolie has not done well he gets degraded to the next rank; a man becomes a woman, a woman a *chokra*; this is a disgrace.

The pluckers come in from up and down the lanes leading to the factory. I like all the colours of the head-shawls gathering together with the pale attractive colour of the baskets and the bright leaf piled inside them. The coolies stop and take out a handful of leaf to show to W. They are proud of their work. Several of the women are champion pluckers and can pluck as much as one hundred to one hundred and twenty pounds a day of Assam leaf and fifty pounds of China.

When the leaf has been weighed, and the coolies paid a pice a pound for anything they have plucked over the agreed amount, it is taken upstairs and the baskets emptied on the withering shelves and spread on their tiers to wither. Now the coolies are free to go.

They go and buy betel leaf and chunam and biris and nuts from the Kyah's man who sits with his tray, like a spider, outside the factory to catch the small flies of pice. Even the smallest lokras are smokers. Then they go away to their villages, smoking and laughing and talking through the late afternoon, and soon, in every hut the smoke goes up and the cows are brought out and milked, the goats and chickens are fed, and the pumpkins are turned on the roof. Soon the firelight shines on gold skins and gold nose-rings and turns the red leeped walls to a deeper mixture of red and gold.

The leaf takes eighteen hours to wither; if it is very wet the hot air is turned on and swept by fans through the rooms. Withering leaf has a peculiar heavy rank smell. When it is

ready, it is dropped down shutes in the floor to the rolling machines that roll it round and round to break the cells and give the necessary twist to the tea leaf.

After that it is fermented on concrete slabs in a cool room, until it is the colour of tobacco; the coarser leaf goes back to be rolled again; it is separated on the jigger, a machine with wire-mesh trays that jiggles the finer leaf through.

Then it is fired. It is put on machines shaped like tanks and drawn backwards on caterpillar rollers into a cavern of hot air that rises from the furnaces; here are stokers and furnace doors clanging and a red-hot light across the floor. After twenty minutes creeping in the inside of the machine, the leaf falls out into troughs on the floor the straight black tea we know.

It is not finished yet. Odorous and hot, it is scooped up with a shovel by boys and wheeled away in barrows. It is not quite cooked; if you crush it in your hand it feels spongy and it goes into a smaller fiercer cooker. Then it is cleaned, sorted, graded and packed. This is all done by hand, except that a gigantic jigger is used and the tea falls out on different sides in its different grades.

There are women sitting on the floor with flat scoop shaped wicker trays sorting, sifting with a side-to-side motion that is skilful and impossible to copy; they can sift all the different sorts of tea to different sides of their trays without ever touching it with their fingers, they can toss an entire tray of tea to another on the floor two yards away in one flash of movement without spilling a leaf.

The colours are beautiful: the women sitting on the gold wood floor, the dirty colours of their working clothes: dull blue, mulberry, dull yellow, and the green bronze grasses they make into sweeping brooms and the piles of black tea.

W. shows us some Flowery Orange Pekoe; some of its leaves are really gold.

W. You couldn't buy that for ten or twelve shillings a pound.

We see the leaf rushing down the valley from Rungjeli in sacks on the ropeway; we see the pack-ponies string in from Chinglam; we see the Munshi delving in the baskets to make sure there are no stones put in to cheat the weight. We see the day's production being weighed, black and redolent, in deep-sided wooden boxes that the boys wheel up on trucks.

The boxes are made in the factory since the war; before, they were imported from Scandinavia and built in the workshops. When they are packed and shut and stencilled they go by pack-pony to the station in the forest to catch the little Himalayan train.

The names of the tea are beautiful too:

Flowery Orange Pekoe.
Orange Pekoe.
Pekoe.

These are whole-leaf grades:

Broken Orange Pekoe.
Broken Pekoe.
Orange Fannings.
Pekoe Fannings.
Souchong.

These are broken grades:

Dust.

This is sold on the internal market for native consumption at five to seven annas a pound.

Last year W. made four hundred and fifty thousand pounds of tea. This year he says he will make half a million.

Dear. . . .
Down the factory, down the village, pick tea up. Sabrina been the factory house. W. gave Sabrina a tiny tin of tea. I did go to office. I did go see tea.
Love and kisses.

Letter from Sabrina, aged 3.

Giovanna has given up trying to curl the children's hair; at least I have asked that she should not try, any more. She contents herself by twisting Henry's round her fingers; it stays to any shape it is put, soft and golden brown. Henry is sure, quite rightly, that he is very beautiful.

Rafael and Sabrina now have coronels: neat smooth plaits banded round their heads and tied together at the tips on their partings with blue plaid bows. They look like midget Austrian waitresses.

If I tell the children stories they always want the stories to be about themselves and the stories always begin: 'Once upon a time there were two girls, one with hair like marmalade and one with hair like honey.'

Indian Summer of a Pekinese.

Old Sol lies out on the drive in the sun. The colourings of his coat exactly match the autumn: the drying grass, the ripening millet, the deep colour of the marigolds and the yellow daisies growing in the crops. A gentle wind sends down a leaf to blow along the drive, a dry irresistible tawny flight that makes his muscles ripple down his flanks, but Candytuft springs out past him to catch it. Sol is benevolent and lets this pass, and the wind and a dozen friendly scents eddy round him and he sinks to sleep.

Yesterday he ran three miles up the river with the ponies, today he has been to the crest of the Saddle, panting madly through the tea bushes, coming back covered in burrs, matted in every feather. His thirteen years lie lightly on his head.

In Calcutta he had rheumatism from the stone floors;

he had lost his last big tooth in a fight and in the evenings lay slowly breaking his heart over his ball that he could no longer pick up. A film had come over his eyes. His temper was irascible and unprintable.

At Chinglam the years slide backwards over his tail; a new springiness flows in his bones, his coat takes on new colours and new depth and though he still fights with young Sol, as is becoming to the stag of the herd, it is in sharp manly satisfactory fight.

Old Sol has a tag of beautiful newness joined to the end of his days.

October 23rd.

The villages have a riper beauty. The poinsettias are out, big long-leafed flowers of so flaming a scarlet that they are flags on the hill. With them are delicate, petalled, broken-white shapes of bauhinia trees. The millet is ripe and the pumpkins are turning yellow.

There is another crop that covers the whole field in tiny pale and deep pink flowers shaped like cherry pie. I pick it for the vases and all the servants laugh. I do not know what crop it is.

When I sit up late to work after Giovanna has gone to bed, in the silence I hear a drum beating. It is oddly frightening, and then, suddenly, I hear it close. I start and the blood runs up my neck . . . but it is only Peter Rabbit stamping on the clay floor of his stall

TONIGHT IS DEWALI, the Feast of Lights.

We have seen it in the city; last year I took Giovanna and the children and we drove through the congested Indian quarters of Calcutta, and saw the lights on every gate and wall and window-ledge and roof, and the processions and the fireworks, and the lights on the boats on the river.

Now we see Dewali in the country. The chief difference is that we see it at a distance; the mountain looks like a city far away; on every path and every hut are lights, shielded somehow from the wind. It looks like a city or like fireflies, and it is not easy to see in the darkness where the mountain ceases and the sky and the stars begin.

Baju comes out and tries to put eight lights in a row along the gong-stand. He cannot do it; he drops them over the edge and Monbad comes out and takes them from him and gets a cuff on the ear. He lets Baju cuff him while he sets six lights in a row on the gong and two on the rock above the drive.

Baju goes reeling away round the corner of the house. He is very drunk tonight and very noisy.

There is an extraordinary contrast between his noise and garrulousness and smell of drink, and the calmness of the little lights burning on the hill. It reminds me of Christmas, how most people treat it, and how it continues to remain in spite of them: lights, night, darkness, dark spruce green, and stars, and children running out to see, and calm and beauty.

I can hear Baju shouting for most of the night.

THE PUPPIES ARE promoted into a play-pen on the lawn. They stumble and totter and fall on their noses in the grass. Bunny is all bone and blackness and obviously twice as clever as he is twice as large as the others; he is precocious. Honey is fat and fair, a small sack of sweetness and fluff. Sunny, the only bitch, is still in the mouse stage and sleeps most of the time.

Henry and Rafael are tormented with fear of the falcons, as they call the chestnut-coloured kites that fly over the gulf.

Rafael. In *Switzerland* falcons take lambs! And babies! They would take the puppies . . . *easily.*

Henry. And I am not very sure about Sabrina.

AS WE GO down to fish in the Teesta river, we see the Snows in a new way, looming one after another into the sky behind the near mountain as we drop down. It is rather like seeing a sailing ship in full canvas coming round a headland. A peak first appears at an incredible distance up in the sky; is it a peak or a cloud, a transfixed cloud? It is Narsing. Then, higher, the next appears, and higher and higher until

Kanchenjunga comes with its twin points looming into the sky and behind it Kabru and Janu, with their snowfields glittering in the sun.

Henry, looking at Kanchenjunga with enormous eyes. Does it go all the way up from the ground to there?

The Teesta is thick, grey-green, swirling into whirlpools and rapids; today it looks what it is, a dangerous cruel swollen river. We leave it and go up the Rungeet that is smaller and more gay, with deep greengage-green water. We lunch by the frontier bridge that leads into Sikkim. It is a thread of a bridge suspended and it sways as the people and pack-ponies go over it one by one; it has a policeman at each end.

All along the banks are bauhinia trees in flower and their petals drop into the sand as we sit.

We fish at the junction of the rivers, where the Rungeet makes a loop of its own water in the muddier colour of the Teesta. We are fishing for mahseer, fish that can go up to 80 pounds or more.

Soon the Teesta will clear and the water will be the blue of an aquamarine. There is a sweep of sand hot from the sun; we rest there and by putting our heads back and back and back we can look up to the tip of Kabru which is the only peak that shows there in the valley.

On the way home we stop in the village of Teesta Bazaar, a big village, and buy beads to take home to Sabrina, who is too young to come. The beads are big blue and white and black ones on a string; they are meant as necklaces for ponies and bullocks to wear, but Sabrina will love them.

Out of the flocks of goats here no one ever takes a drop of milk. I want some goats' milk to make cheese and the servants assure me that I cannot get it.

'But what do you do with the milk? What is the milk for?'

After some thought they reply that it is for the kids.

It is strange the significance that white always plays for me, especially here at Chinglam. Chinglam has so many white flowers; the native ones, wild coffee, and tree daisies that are just coming into bud, cosmos and half-wild white roses. There are white snows and white clouds and the white animals, the white pony and white pekinese; even the newest chicken to come out of the egg is white.

The servants give me presents. Ears' two eldest children come, dressed in their best clothes; apricot cross-draped robes, white blouses, red pigtail ties on hair oiled with coconut oil to such glossiness that I wonder how the ties keep on. They give me a bowl of eggs, eggs are an especially polite present, and a whole branch of bananas and a platter of broad beans in crimson pods. Then Monbad's wife and mother bring me two beer bottles full of milk and a dish of oranges decorated with green leaves and a bunch of roses.

Lena marches in and puts down a plate of small rarer oranges like mandarins.

Lena. For dressing my bad heel and for saying goodbye.

She bursts into tears. Tears come out of her hard little eyes and stream down her cheeks. Tomorrow she is to go away with Henry.

Is Lena really nicer? Or do I only think so because she has begun to like me?

We take Giovanna and Henry and Lena down to the station.

It is the orange season and thousands and thousands of oranges are brought from the groves in the valleys as far as Sikkim to every station on the line. We meet oranges all along the road, carried in big baskets; the coolies who carry them have a stick like a crutch and when they need to rest they put the crutch under the bottom of the heavy basket on their backs and support themselves as if they had three legs, while they pant and the sweat drips off their shoulders and heads.

The men who are buying the oranges are foreign to this district, dark men with huge moustachios; I think they are Rajputs. They come for the season and each has his sorters and packers and carpenters, who sort and pack the oranges and make the boxes in the station yard. Coolies come backwards and forwards, bringing loads of wood, seers of nails, loads of newspapers, and oranges and oranges and oranges, in their cone-shaped baskets.

The packers are all women and the newspapers are all American; the *Los Angeles Times* and the *San Francisco Gazette*. Giovanna nearly misses the train, we are so engrossed reading them; she reads advertisements for *'young steer beef at 15c. a lb.'* and I read a strip about a comic sheriff. The press mystifies Giovanna, who finds it hard enough to talk English, let alone American.

It is time for the evening meal and a great deal of cooking and eating is going on all up and down the piece of ground that is the platform; fires burn among flat stones with pots made of iron or brass cooking on them, very odorous cooking. People are sitting round a platter, four or five at a time and dipping with their hands. When they finish they rinse their mouths in a lota of water and spit it out among the bushes, but they regurgitate long after that.

Henry, longingly. Why is it only polite for us to spit when we do our teeth?

The noises of the train comes a long while before it, but at last we see it and the late sunlight gleaming on its brass funnel. Lena, Henry, Rafael and Giovanna all begin to cry. I could cry too.

It is sad going home, but first a barking deer springs out and runs in front of the car, and then a jungle cock and two hens walk leisurely across the road in front of us.

We tell them to take Henry's bed out of the nursery and put it into the godown. We cannot bear to see it; it still has his name heart on it. Everywhere are bowls of flowers that Giovanna arranged before she left.

She has gone and a great stillness has fallen on the house and the garden and the valley. Do I hate it? Yes, I think I do.

I TAKE THE children for walks and I notice that whenever the coolies see them they break into small soft murmurs, especially with Sabrina. It is her hair.

Sabrina's hair is thick, heavy and pale, pale gold. It is very wonderful by coolie standards. It hangs straight to her shoulders in a thick roll, falling down straight each side of her face that is narrow and pointed with beautiful deep eyes. Her features are strongly marked and marked by temper as well. She is either going to be hideous or beautiful.

I LEAVE MY work and the children and go up to the Viewpoint to see if the sunset will turn the snows red.

The road leads between two worlds, the ridge of the Viewpoint, and Chinglam. Chinglam is a world of valleys, mountain folds and ridges, floating with clouds, and with its river embedded at its foot. It is all enclosed by mountains. The Viewpoint is open, open to the great Snows, to the Kanchenjunga range and the Sikkim snows that are not snowed at all now but faint pellucid blue, with snow streaks on them.

This part of the garden is more beautifully set than any other; it runs from a height in the sky to its winding lower road and it sometimes has the look of the landscapes in the background of a Filippino Lippi picture. It is spread on the side of the hill, it undulates and rises, catching the light with every shade of greenness and it is planted with cherry trees. The old manager, before W., had an idea that in time they would taste the tea: blend it with cherry, give it a cherry tang. W. says he does not believe it, but I have heard other managers say that if sal trees are planted with tea, they will give it a taste of almonds.

The top boundary here is the sky and the other side of the ridge, above Chinglam, is a sheer precipice. Walking along the ridge you look on one side down at Chinglam and its river and clouds, and on the other across, and far up, to the Snows.

As I walk along, the gong rings and the coolies pass me on their way into the factory. They pass under the bright green leaves of the cherry trees and the colours of their clothes fit the earth; singly, the colours are ugly and dull, together they are lovely; blues and duns and dirty whites, heliotropes and pinks and blacks against the sunbaked earth. All the coolies stop to laugh at the dogs. They laugh at their flat noses and I laugh because they have the identical noses themselves. Sabrina and I are the only people on Chinglam with anything like a nose. I hear them still laughing as they go away and afterwards I hear a flute. It goes further and further away until I cannot hear it any more.

I am quite alone on the hill; it is cold and the shade trees have the shape of winter; they are bare, their twigs black and a pale birch silver shines on their trunks.

The dogs whine to go home, but I stay. The snows do go red: first yellow—then gold, not yellow—real pink-red. I leave them red and run all the way home.

At Chinglam I love to come home. I like to see from far off the white walls shining in the surrounding green and the lamplight, my lamplight, beaming under the stars. I have never seen such a vault of starlight as the night sky over this valley; it seems wider than anywhere else and, in the cold, the stars are enormous and the Chinglam trees seem to heighten and brush the stars with their dark shapes.

As I walk towards the house, all over the valley are sounds: a flute, a cow, a very small bell ringing in a very small temple, a cooking-pot being scoured with mud, water running into a tin.

The servants run to meet me with a lantern and I can tell

who they are by the white shapes of their clothes. I cannot see Sol, nor young Sol now, but Comfort and Candytuft coming to meet me, gleam like swans' feathers as they run.

There is a smell of hay and wet earth from the watered beds.

'Who watered the beds? Did Baju? I told him to.'

A silence. A hesitation.

A voice from the shadows. Your honour ... I watered them.

'It is the garden-boy's day to go to the post. Why should he come back and do Baju's work?'

Why? Because Baju is too drunk to do it himself. They know, and I know, and they know that I know. We do not say any more, but soon I shall have to report Baju to W.

I go into the house. It smells of floor polish and burning logs and the close sweet-smelling roses in the Bristol bowls.

In the nursery the cloth is spread and the lamp is lit; its light falls in a circle, shutting out the friendly toys and containing Rafael, Sabrina and a little of Ayah, who stands half in it and half out. Rafael and Sabrina are eating bread and butter and sugar like the children in a fairytale and their coronels of red and golden hair are like wreaths. They have been to the leaf shed to see the leaf weighed and they were weighed themselves.

Rafael. The Munshi gave us bananas off his own tree and he showed us his pigeons. We carried the bananas home in

Ayah's veil. I weigh twenty-two seers and Sabrina weighs twelve.

Sabrina who weighs twelve seers is too busy eating to say a word.

I get a letter addressed to: Miss Sodden, Gin Glam.

EVERY MORNING AT seven the coolies go up to the tool-house at the end of our garden to fetch their tools, their baskets for plucking, the little curved sickles they use for cutting the undergrowth, their mattocks and hoes and water-tins. Baju is always there to give these out; if he were not he would be reported to W. He counts the tools by putting marks on the wall. The procession of coolies start with their foreman to the lot to be picked.

'Where are you picking?'

'Oh, we are picking Chinglam.'

'Where are you cleaning?'

'Oh, we are cleaning Chinglam.'

The head-shawls and the baskets go down the hill and the drab colours of the men go with them and the peculiar nasal songs float back to the house. These songs are like the flute, always slightly sad; they seem to me to go back in origin through Mongolia to the Steppes. Perhaps they do. They might.

The coolies sing mostly in the evenings, after the leaf is

plucked and weighed and taken away. They come back up the hill to give in their tools and sing out into the quiet colours of the evenings.

November.

It is getting colder. Michaelmas daisies come out in the garden with the first sweet-peas and cornflowers and poinsettias. In this mixture of English summer flowers and Indian, there is an authentic touch of autumn.

We give a Guy Fawkes party. It is attended by W. and M., Rafael, Sabrina and I and perhaps five hundred uninvited coolies who sit on the bank and watch. I do not think they have ever seen fireworks, and they were sure that the Guy on the bonfire was Hitler.

Dear . . .

We gathered a big sack of shavings but they were only a little on our huge big bonfire. Monbad and the garden boy and the new woodcutter and the grass-cutter made the bonfire. Guy Fawkes was burnt up at once and then we did let the bonfire get littler and littler and we put fireworks and the rockets went into the bushes of tea quite often instead of into the sky; some went into the coolies but they did only laugh. Then we had bangs and then we had beautiful fireworks shooting up like silver fountains and then we did roast potatoes and we went in and ate beautiful roast potatoes and butter and salt. I have put all that I can remember out of my head and now I have nothing more so I shall go.'

Letter from Rafael.

'And the apples were tookened for nothing because they wouldn't roast.'

Sabrina.

A WILD MAN and a wild BOY come to beg. They are Bhutias with skins like Red Indians and Chinese faces, more animal and merry and stupid than the faces of most Chinese, but as enduring. Their robes have become a pelt with grease and lice; the man's is turned back leaving his body cold to the air and his hair is in ropes like the shepherds we saw before the Pujas; the boy's hair is in wolf locks but his eyes, as he looks at our unfamiliarity, are wistful as if he would like to take a little of our strangeness away and keep it forever. They have one ear-ring each, the size of a bracelet, silver, and meeting in a turquoise. They have the beautiful knee-high patchwork padded boots I saw in Darjeeling.

I try to talk to them but fail. Rafael does better. She goes in and brings out one of the lollipops Henry sent her. She gives it to the boy. He cannot understand it. He turns it over and over in his hands like a monkey and finally puts it away in his pouch, that is not in his cheek like a monkey's, but in the front of his robe. His eyes are gay and hard now, like a monkey's too, with no trace of feeling. He has what he wanted.

IT IS CURIOUS how being alone seems to have given me a new power of love; perhaps, as with everything else, I have more time to think about it; perhaps I like people better when they are not there. I remember, disturbingly, a reviewer of my third book who said: '*one thing people may not like about this book is its self-content . . . there is a quality about it which seems to say that it is about people because it must be and that the author really likes things better than people. Likes them for their own sakes as a miser likes gold.*'

Is it true? But my love for the people I love seems heightened: I can feel it growing and living.

I have always distrusted the word 'burgeoning'. I look it up in the dictionary. 'To burgeon—to grow—put forth buds—or sprouts.' I can only hope that mine are buds.

DID YOU KNOW that tea has flowers like camellias? Tiny wax ones with a splash of gold in the centre? Why has not anyone mentioned them? It is true that they grow on the under-sides of the bushes and the top of the bush is cut to an even spread of green, table-pruned, so that you hardly see them, but they are there and balls of fruit as well.

Did you know that clouds lie far below us in the sun and do not melt away? Lie all day in a curl of white hiding the river?

In the night it is so still now that I can hear the waterfalls loudly in my room and often, from some village far away, the beating of a drum.

We go out with W. and pass the wild men's camp. They have leaf tents and several fires in the stones and a herd of donkeys, all young and black, eating wild sunflowers and turning blunt babyish faces to look at the car.

We pass a coolie leaning his load against a tea bush. W. speaks to him but with no sign of temper.

'What did you say to him, W.?'

W. pleasantly. I said: 'God rot your soul. You are spoiling in five seconds what took me five years to grow.'

Thinking of W., a tea garden manager must be a mixture of unusual things. He must be a born agriculturalist with an itch to make things grow; that must be his first desire. Then he must be a squire with a squire's understanding and biased fondness for his own particular village and his villagers, though Rungolo is large for a village; it has five hundred and fifty houses, more than three thousand coolies, three hundred and fifty cows, eleven hundred goats, fifty-one pack-ponies and twenty sheep. No one has ever counted the hens.

W. has to know them all and know about them all. He has to be a business man, the correspondence and organisation are his to handle; he has to deal with labour and labour problems. He has to be mechanically minded enough to supervise his factory machinery and electric plants and lorries and cars, when he had lorries and cars. He has often to be a doctor and says he has been a midwife. He has to speak the language, almost to think in the language, and, coming back to the beginning, he has to be a countryman with a countryman's ability to lose himself in the country and stay there for long stretches of loneliness and boredom. The rains at Rungolo last for three-and-a-half months and it is often cut off in that time, even from the post.

As for being balanced enough to take all his power with a pinch of salt, not many managers can do it; tea-planting is full of cranks and oddities and lop-brained fanatics. Many of the Assistants go home because they cannot bear the loneliness. Chinglam has had that effect on some of them. To me its loneliness has been like a charm.

WHEN PETER RABBIT came the sparrows came as well. They treat the house as theirs and fly into the store-room and pick the grain out of the bags. They hardly bother to move when I give out the horse food. The house is full of chirpings and the children's and sparrows' voices seem inextricably mixed and almost equally loud.

We have decided to get another pony. It is coming soon.

Sabrina. I don't want a mother pony. I don't want a daddy one either. I want one the same little as me.

The huge young water-carrier wants to join the army. It is a good thing as, though he is willing and merry, he is very full-blooded and turbulent and there is always trouble with him in the servants' quarters.

This will make thirty-six gone from Chinglam. The bread-runner is worried because the recruit, his son, does not write. He could if he wished because there are letter-writers in every regiment, but I think he does not want to send money home and I am afraid it is for the money and not for news that the bread-runner is so anxious.

There are notices pasted up, and I saw them at the forest station. 'All men of the -th Gurkha Regiment at present on leave, to join their units immediately.' It was repeated in dialect.

Conversation 4.

Rafael. Why didn't you have a boy instead of girls?

'Never mind. You grow up and have a little boy and I shall look after him.'

Rafael, surprised. But you won't be able to. Then you will be dead.

There is a small house on the ridge beyond Chinglam at the edge of the tea that fascinates me. It is on the edge of the tea; first it looks at the mountains and beyond them it looks at the plains where the Teesta appears to flow into pools; they look like limpid puddles, so near and so clear that you could step into them. It can also see our own small Runglee river below the chincona hills and it can see a loop of the Teesta that has now taken its winter colour of blue.

This house has a hedge of poinsettias and three terraced fields about the size of three large carpets; they are sown with the pink flowering crop and have an outcrop of sunflowers,

yellow in the pink. It has a stack of Indian corn in sheaf that is stored on a tall tripod of bamboos, and the ends of the tripod end in bunches of marigolds.

I like to see this house in the evenings at dusk when it sits into the sunset, when the clouds lie above the fields and take the colours of the crops.

An apple man comes, a Sikkimese, in an old mulberry robe with pale blue linings and sleeve-cuffs and delightful brass buttons that have their heads carved into flowers.

He has only one pound weight so that he weighs a pound of apples and then puts them into the weighted side of the scales, and weighs two pounds of apples to make a seer. We weigh apples against apples until I buy a maund of red sweet Sikkim apples.

He has tree tomatoes too, globular, with skins like Victoria plums and flesh like peaches. They taste delicious but have a tang of their own. He came on a chestnut pony that has small curls all over it and a necklace of beads.

I ask him to bring me some buttons like his. He says no, he cannot come again it is too far. After a minute he says he may come.

The little new skewbald pony, after staggering eighteen miles, staggered into the stable that we had made for it. There was grass and a bran mash waiting and it did not know which to eat first; it looked as if it were months since it had seen either and it ate snatches of both, lashing round with its head if anyone came near it and shivering if anyone spoke. When it had eaten it fell down and went to sleep.

It is simply a heap of bones in wrinkled parti-coloured skin. The servants come out to see it one by one and give their verdict on it; the bread-runner thinks it will do; Monbad says it is not worth forty rupees which is what I have paid for it, and Kokil says it will die. Kokil always predicts illness and disaster in a crisis, but he always helps to keep both away. He works hard with me over the pony.

I go to see it later. It is still asleep in the straw, with the moonlight streaming over it. Its head looks oddly trustful and young. I hope suddenly, for its own sake instead of mine, that it does not turn out to be a swindle, too old to be worth keeping or with a temper that is not only from cruel handling but in its character.

When i meet coolies on these narrow paths they come steadily on towards me. Sometimes they salaam and sometimes they ignore me politely. Always after they have passed, there is a smell of old clothes pickled in woodsmoke and sweat and a stronger smell of *biris*. At first I hated this, now it is familiar, almost, even though it is so strong, friendly.

We go to see the new pony in the morning. Its brown and white sides look hollow and miserably rough.

Rafael. I want to call it Beauty.

'It looks more like "Fright" to me.'

Rafael, shocked. Hush! You must not say unkind things like that where it can hear you.

Sabrina, peering at it. It's a *plaid* pony!

Writing my poem in my head all afternoon as I walk on the Saddle, I can see how little attached the poet is to the world in one sense, how detached, and how deeply attached he is in another. Though I am in the poem, far away with it, I am very much in the evening too. As soon as it grows dark at Chinglam now, the mountains seem to recede and the sky to widen; the valley is quite lost except for the sound of the stream. The sky tonight is a luminous blue, with the light and the pink in it that you find in an opal, while the hills darken from olive, to green as dark as black. Below Chinglam, the tree daisies make a foam that is romantic in the dusk; they are tall, ten feet high, but their heads are on a level with the lawn; they look like a cherry orchard and bring a queer nostalgic Russian feeling.

I feel the world of Chinglam in this way this evening, but I am removed from it as a poet is: out of touch, out of sense, and yet has it all in the hollow of his hand. A poet could bring it all back in the margin of a few words. How? I do not know. I am not a poet. I only feel like one sometimes. I only know what his feelings would be.

There are two cycles of work on a tea-garden. The first is the pruning cycle and it may extend over as much as twenty-five years. They say a manager prunes, not for the manager after him, but for the manager after that. Every planter, including W., has his own unshakable theory about pruning; it is extremely important and may make thousands of rupees' difference on the crop. The second cycle is the cycle of the year and it comes with a rhythmical repetition year after year and always will come as long as tea is grown.

The Tea Year really begins with the First Flush which comes about March 20th and leads to a rush of plucking and manufacturing for about a month. The Second Flush starts in May and lasts into July and this is the quality period when quality tea is made. After that, quality declines and Rains Tea is made until the Autumnals come from the middle of October to the middle of November. The winter is given to pruning and manuring, top-dressing, re-terracing where the rains have eaten the earth away, cut-back pruning when the bushes are cut to the roots, and spraying. In February, bamboos and thatch are cut and time given for repairing of houses and making new ones and refencing. This goes on until the First Flush comes again in March and it all begins again.

W. says it turns round almost as quickly as the Buddhist prayer wheel turns in the stream.

Visitors come to see me. They express, first surprise, and then sympathy that I should live here alone. The same thing happens every time, the rare times, people come here or I meet them at W. and M.'s; surprise and sympathy. 'I think you are very brave,' says the doctor who comes to look at Rafael's tonsils. 'How lonely you must be!' 'Don't you find the evenings awful?' 'How can you bear all these coolies?' 'How do you get to the Club?' say the visitors.

I try to explain that I do not need to be brave; that I am not lonely; that I do not like going to the Club, and that I like my evenings working and reading in my room, with the children asleep next door and the dogs asleep in their baskets; with the smell of the bowls of my own sweet-peas, and the smell of the sap in the logs; and outside the dome of the Chinglam sky where, these nights of moonlight, the stars seem small and far away and the tree daisies loom near and large.

I try to explain and then I do not try. Rafael and Sabrina and I show the visitors round; we show them the garden and the view to the west, and the view to the east, and Rafael shows them the new chicken-house and her row of salads. It seems quickly done and perhaps to them there is little to show, but tacitly, there is so much that we do not show; we do not speak to them about the Saddle and the Viewpoint for instance, nor the little house with the flowering crop, nor the pool. We take them in and give them tea and we know quite well what they will admire: Candytuft and the Nanking bowls and Sabrina's eyes. Rafael stands and smiles uncertainly; I wish they would, just for once, admire hers.

Then they go. It is quiet. Ears washes up the extra tea things and Ayah comes in and gently puts them back in their place along the mantelpiece. Kokil sweeps up the hearth with a broom of grasses and old Sol, who is too cross for company, is let out of the office and rushes up and down the lawn. Sabrina goes to have her bath and Rafael casts herself down on the carpet.

Rafael. I'm tired. They're gone. Let's read.

Letters to Giovanna

'. . . .

I had a sausage roll. I had a telegram from England. I play with my baby so beautifully. She was born again yesterday. I pretend I have not had her for years and years. Babies can be born again, can't they?'

Rafael.

'. . . .

I like to do sewing. I want to see Giovanna. Very big girl now. No milk for breakfast any more— porridge.'

Sabrina.

NOVEMBER 30TH.

From, the top of the Saddle and down the paths early this morning comes the sound of a flute.

'What is it, Ayah?'

Ayah. It is picnic puja.

She does not know its proper name. Perhaps it has not got one, perhaps it is only a picnic and picnics here are ritual ones. They start with a small procession winding out of a village; men walking in front, women walking behind; the children seem to be left at home. One of the men in each procession has a flute and more of them have drums; the melodies cross one another up the mountain and the drum-beats collide gently as they are beaten, one procession against another.

They go up to the Saddle. They have music and flowers and drink and they will stay there all day. The drink is carried in a kerosene tin on a man's back; he is the only one who walks soberly. The drinking glasses are wide bamboos about a foot long and cut off at a join that makes a bottom; they are slung on a bamboo-bark handle. Everyone has their own food tied in a cloth, but there is far more drink than food. Some carry two or three fronds of sugarcane and the green leaves, like branches of palm, give the procession a sacred air. Some of the women have bunches of poinsettia, they all have poinsettia flowers and marigold; the flowers and the bright green sugar-cane and the colours of the skirts and head-veils go winding up the hill. We can see the colours long after the sound of the music is lost.

Then suddenly the sound of the music comes again. The beats seem to fall out of the sky and now the procession is up on the Saddle and the people have planted flags in the wind. They stay there all day while the picnic people make music and love, and drink and eat. At four o'clock they come down. The sun has gone from the valley and the music comes near and goes away again as the processions wind backwards and forwards along the zigzag paths that cross the mountain in the tea. One by one the flutes and the drums stop as the villages are reached and the people go into their homes.

Some of the coolies who do not approve, have spent the day cutting wood by the river or cutting grain or simply washing; washing is simple; you sit in the stream and take off all your clothes except an undershirt or skirt and thump your clothes in the water with a stick. It is simple, but very cold.

It is almost winter. The sunflowers are going over, dark gold, and the Teesta is its true winter colour, aquamarine or zircon blue. The mornings are frosty. The water is like ice. W. says most of the coolies will not wash now till the spring.

They are dirty. I saw a woman selling biris by the leaf shed; she was striking and I stared at her for a long while before I saw what was the matter with her: she was clean. It was like an advertisement for Persil.

They are not as dirty as Tibetans and Bhutias who do

not change their clothes sometimes for a year. Nepalis wash, at any rate in the summer, and girls who want to get married wash all the year round. The mothers wash the children occasionally; I saw a Nepali mother brushing her child's hair with a little twig broom.

In early December the lower hills have bright scarlet foliage in their woods; this is from the pillilli trees; they are tall and scarlet-leafed, rather like I imagine maples to be when they have turned.

The flowers here are mixed in the same ways as the fruit: sunflowers and marigolds and roses and poinsettias are out together, out of their true seasons, and daisies and dahlias grow on trees.

The apple man comes back. He says he has brought me some of the buttons I asked for, but he says they are very expensive and looks at me as if he is afraid they are too costly for me to take. I ask how much they are. They are twelve annas for five. I try to make a face that is suitably impressed and ask to see them. He produces them out of the pouch of his robe; packets of white paper written over in Tibetan characters; inside each packet is a square two inches of magenta silk and five buttons; they are shaped like peardrops and the heads are carved with a flower or a rough Phoenix or a Chinese pattern. I take all thirty and some small ones for Rafael's coat.

The apple man says he has his daughter with him and she would like to sell me some peas. I look up the drive and down the garden and say, where is she? He says she is very shy. Presently she comes out slowly from behind a tree. She has a basket of peas and tree tomatoes and the colour of the pods looks wonderfully fresh against the wallflower brown velvet of her robe; she has cream sleeves and a red sash and her hair is in a pigtail braided with scarlet nearly to her knees. She does not look up, she looks down, and her eyelids make two small upturned crescent shapes on her cheeks and her skin is the blend of red and pink and brown of the skins of the tree tomatoes. As soon as she has shown her basket, she retires behind the tree again.

I buy all she has.

Rafael. If I had any money do you know what I should buy? A picture of the big snows and a little private spoon.

December 4th.

Things will not happen by themselves. Unless you start them and work at them and go on working at them, they will not happen. Even thunderbolts are electricity and not acts of God. *Also* you must remember that people do not usually keep their promises. You must not expect it. Think how difficult it is to keep your own and then you will see how unlikely it is that they will keep theirs.

I CAME BACK to the small house I like, and the crop in the field that was pink has turned sorrel red.

All over the hill are these patches of sorrel and the millet is being cut, leaving pale silver stalks and stubble where the crop has been.

In our own garden the jasmine bushes have flowered into small canary yellow flowers that tumble off into the grass quickly and look better there. I have told the garden-boy not to sweep them up; he is too gentle to say so but he thinks I am peculiar.

What has come out in the garden?

Cornflowers, of course. Cornflowers everywhere, in every bed; *and* the portuluca that Giovanna raked up. No other portuluca has come out at all in spite of the green carpets under the roses. In honesty I have to write and tell her this and she answers, 'Allora, vale auche essere una zocchola—then an old wooden shoe can also be valuable!' on a postcard.

When M. comes to see me I am ashamed of my beds so full of mistakes that are blank and have not come up or mistakes that have come up too much and have not flowered, and all the other sorts of mistakes. It is more mysterious because the same seedlings, from the same seeds, have turned M.'s garden into a paradise. The garden-boy and I are scalding with shame as M. and W. walk along the beds.

M. says, 'I think you have done wonders': and she praises the cornflowers and the turrets of sweet-peas and the size of the petunias round the porch. I see W. looking curiously at the creeping green without a flower, of the portuluca, as if he were wondering if it is a new kind of moss or a vegetable, but he says nothing and 'I think you have done *wonderfully*,' says M.

Comfort has decided to wean her puppies; Honey and Sunny are agreeable but Bunny is not. As he can run now nearly as fast as Comfort and is nearly as large, it is difficult. If he is penned he howls like a jackal, if he is loose he bites like a weasel. Comfort looks haggard and old Sol looks disgusted and young Sol thinks he will fight. I decide to despatch Bunny to his new home.

The plaid pony is visibly fattening and sweetening.

December 8th.

War with Japan.

M. comes over and we have a curious difficulty in keeping warm. Everything has a renewed sharpness. We discuss the possibility of having refugees. The difficulties at Chinglam are water, light because of the shortage of oil, and food.

Nobody comes. I think the railways will be swamped immediately by the wealthy Marwaris panicking away.

The children come to me.

Rafael. For a *great* treat can Sabrina and I go for a picnic without you?

When I come to think it over I am pleased. The more they are self-sufficient, the better for me. I revel in them; Rafael is dear, not only to me, and Sabrina is sometimes beautiful, but I like it when they leave me alone. I revel too, more and more, in my solitude.

When I first came I was not used to it. The solitariness of Chinglam is not extreme but to some people I suppose it would be like a spell of solitary confinement. At first it made me uneasy, I found myself listening to it, and it made me depressed; then I began to learn.

In good company your thoughts run, in solitude your thought is still; it goes deeper and makes for itself a deeper groove, delves. Delve means 'dig with a spade'; it means hard work. In talk your mind can be stretched, widened, exhilarated to heights but it cannot be deepened; you have to deepen it yourself.

It needs sturdiness. You will be lonely, you will be depressed; you must expect it; if you were training your body it would ache and be tired. It is worth it. There is a Hindu proverb which says: 'You only grow when you are alone'.

The best would be to have friends who came and went away; but if I had to choose between their never coming, or never going away, I think I would choose them not to come.

Rafael and Sabrina go out with a basket for a picnic by themselves, three hundred yards into the vast world of tea. When they are gone the house is quiet; only the sunlight shortens on the floor as the afternoon moves, and Baju rings the gong, and there is the sound of water spraying as the garden-boy waters the flowers. Monbad comes in with a tray of tea; Monbad comes in with the letters; presently, in the next room, he lights the fire. At dusk I get up from my desk and stretch, and I hear children and dogs running down the drive, and we meet again, refreshed.

THERE IS ONE thing I have noticed about these coolies: the delight they seem to take in relieving themselves in any prominent view-point. The highest rocks facing the snows are covered in faeces. I wonder if it is a form of self-expression, of assertion, in the face of the overwhelming space.

At any rate it is very tiresome.

THEY TELL ME there is a blind beggar at the door. Automatically I say: 'Tell him to go away.' They go to tell him.

Rafael. He hopped all the way here on one leg.

Suddenly I remember where I am. He must have come at least four miles down this sunbaked steep precipitous way and there are four miles back, uphill, and nothing on the way but the Kyah's shop and the Kyah will give nothing to anyone.

When I come out he is gone. I see him shambling up through the tea, slowly feeling his way in a long dragging olive-coloured serge coat and a black Jew's hat. He carries one hand palm up in front of him. I know it is only from habit; he has held his hand out for money so long that it stays of itself like that, but in the distance it looks as if it is turned up to feel the light.

The garden-boy is thinning out cornflowers. 'Take this money and go after the beggar man.'

The garden-boy looks up.

The garden-boy. The one whose eyes did not see?

His own beautiful eyes kindle with amusement; the blind man's eyes are simply funny and interesting to him.

'Yes, run.'

He runs and comes back not even out of breath.

Garden-boy. He is pleased. He blesses the Memsahib.

And he gracefully folds his legs under him and goes on pulling up cornflowers.

Enormous earth works are going on in the garden. Not only on this but on other gardens near. I went over to one of them riding on Peter, and I saw children, *lokras* doing this work and it made me glad that W. does not encourage anything smaller than a *chokra* to work here. The work is hard; the children carry baskets of earth on their backs and gradually whole terraces appear, new hills, new contours; whole landscapes are cleared away; it made me think of ants. More than ants though, it made me think of Factory Acts and sweated labour. Earth is heavy and some of the children were small. This is the first time I have ever heard children's feet patter, I know they are supposed to patter but usually they do not: they scamper or tread, much like other people's, but these children's, on the hard bare earth with a load on top of them, pattered busily, to get the weight off their backs as soon as possible, and because the foreman was watching them.

At Chinglam the children run to greet W., rather than hurry away from him and there is nothing much smaller than eleven working at Chinglam. 'O'e, Nannie!' says W. to a small girl, and the little Nannie smiles at him out of the corners of her slit eyes and runs on down the path with her basket bobbing on her back. A baby, anything small, is called a Nannie in Paharia, including a small girl.

There is also, here at Chinglam, an intensive spraying going on. For some time I have noticed, on the bushes, that the spines of the leaves look red; they are covered with an infinitesimal red spider. If it is not killed quickly it will spoil a whole expanse of tea. It is sprayed with a solution called Wiz.

It really is Wiz. The sprayers stand in the tea, the sprays in their hands and a kerosene tin full of Wiz on their backs, and the children keep up the supply running backwards and forwards with other kerosene tins on their backs, with a bamboo stem stuffed in the hole to prevent the Wiz bouncing out as they run.

The air is full of squeakings, almost as high as a bat's, from the sprays, and of laughing and jostling and tin noises from the children. I do not think any Factory Acts are needed on W.'s garden.

December 12th

In the bamboo glade by the Saddle, the grass is filled with a wild flower like a Canterbury bell; in the distance it fills the glade with colour and a fictitious look of England, of bluebells; but the wood is unmistakably a bamboo wood, with chequered bamboo stems and translucent green light reflected between them that I should know anywhere as bamboo.

We make lists for Christmas; they are written down and spoken up the chimney; then they are thrown into the flame and, if you are lucky, taken up the chimney on the wind.

Rafael. Please may I have:

Some clothes for my baby, a needlework machine to make clothes for my baby and a fluffy winter coat for my baby.

And please, myself wants, some new handkerchiefs, and a warm little jumper for my baby.

And a little chair for my baby to sit on.

And a little piano too small to really play and some little books of music.

Thank you, Father Christmas.

Sabrina. Please, Christmas, I want:

A new dolly, Pink.
A cooking cooker.
Rafael's cooking pots.
A squirrel like on my pyjamas and
A bear like on my pyjamas.

Thank you. Please.

Sabrina. What *is* Father Christmas.

Rafael, firmly. A very good idea.

December 15th.

We spend the morning at the Viewpoint, the Teesta river thousands of feet below us on one side, the snows thousands of feet above us on the other. We watch the tiny ropeway going across the hills; it is so clear that we can see the scarlet pylons and the gleam of the cables, and the bales travelling along them on their hooks. We can see the Teesta flowing from shade to sun and sun to shade, ice green, jewel blue, with white on the rapids. We lie on our backs on the grass and all round us is sky and there are two butterflies, copper ones, mating and flying in circles; they have all the room in the world. There is nothing else here living but they and us.

If we roll on our sides we can see the cherry trees going back and back the way we have come, and the path growing smaller and smaller like a doll's path in the tea.

The snows are clear. Pandim is blue, not white, and Kanchenjunga itself is only streaked with snow; but there is a blizzard blowing off it that looks like a puff of sugar going into the sky and the wind that blows to us is iced though it is gentle; gently iced, like an iced drink.

THE PICNICS HAPPEN every Sunday now, and the day is full of patterns of sound winding in and out of one another as the processions go up the mountain. The processions are a little like the journey of the Elephant's Child across Africa; they take bananas (but not the little red kind) and sugar-cane (the long purple kind) and melons (the green crackly kind) and they eat the melons and throw the rind about.

They picnic into the early hours of the night tonight, but I agree that it is a night not to go to bed on; the moonlight is so strong and the air is so still that the scent of the roses comes into the rooms. All the same I go to bed, and to sleep.

I shall be thirty-four on Wednesday and that is a bit old for moons.

Two little snails go creeping through the tea: one is Ayah, the other is Sabrina. One wears a plaid shawl, one wears plaid hair ribbons, and both are knitting; Ayah on pins with khaki wool, Sabrina on two sticks with no wool at all.

I feel divided like this valley; part of me is steadily here, the part that orders lunch and makes marmalade and remembers the chickens and plans for Christmas and Sabrina's manners, and hears the reading lesson, but this is down under mist, almost subconscious; it is suddenly broken through sharply, and then I feel poignantly. Small things break it: when Candytuft looks at me and obediently spits out the goat berry as I order him to; a remark of the children's; a letter; but most of it is mist. Next there are folds and folds of uneasy hills, all the war news and war worries in my mind; they loom so large they block out the snows.

The snows are my own, my secret snows. I know they are there; they are only hidden by the hills, behind the clouds. It is only that they are hidden, lost in the cloud; only that I have not seen them for days.

DECEMBER 19TH.

The garden-boy and I count what is the garden: sweet-peas, mignonette just coming into flower, a few violets, tree daisies, bougainvillea and roses; there have been roses ever since we came here, from July to December; the blue bowls are full of them as I write.

We do not try and count the cornflowers.

THERE WAS A funeral on the Ridge today. It was silent except that at the end, a horn was blown. Only two notes, but they fitted a funeral better than any march or bugle I have known. The notes were long, a little hoarse because they were so largely human, melancholy and completely final. They were blown from the top of the Ridge straight into the sky.

THE NEWS OF Hongkong. I had at last to explain to Rafael how I felt. Nothing but her tact and good temper prevented a scene. Can you have tact and good temper at five years old? She has.

IN PLACES ON the garden where they are cutting back the bushes, the tea has the look of a Japanese print after they have finished. It is pruned to the ground, whitened wood stalks and stumps, repeating over and over again on a brown earth background; they look like Japanese writing. Why Japanese and not Chinese I do not know, but it is unmistakably Japanese.

There is a coolie boy sitting on the wall and he, by accident, has Japanese colours on too; the blue of his coat is the blue of a print and the wicker of his basket is a print brown. On the mound above him, where the wind from the plains and the wind from the snows, warm winds and cold winds, will blow them, are four prayer flags. I like to see them.

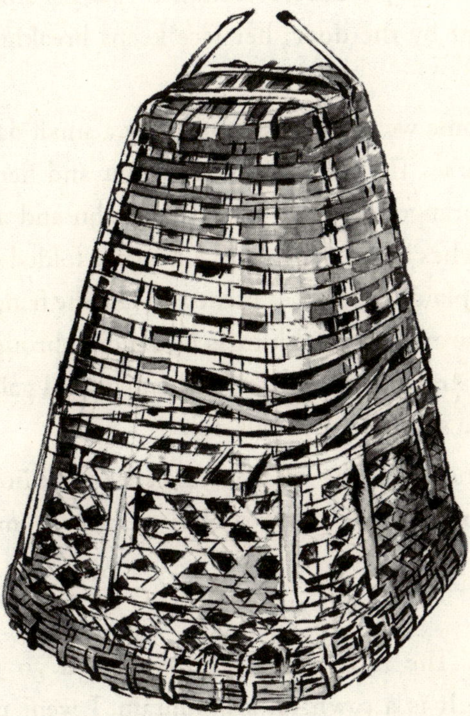

Rafael and I go up to Darjeeling to shop. It is bitterly cold and the small hill streets are almost deserted, but Rafael and I are nearly overcome with excitement at seeing shops again. We go into the Viennese confectioner's for hot coffee, but Rafael finds she is so excited that nothing can go down.

We go into the market to buy presents for the servants' children, and we go into the European shops to look at crackers, but crackers are impossible for us this year. We go to order our Christmas cake and I have to leave Rafael outside because I want to keep it a secret from her. I see her shivering with excitement by the door; her face keeps breaking into smiles.

Coming home we pass a Punjabi riding a small dappled mettlesome horse. The Punjabi looks gallant and fierce, he wears a huge orange turban of swathed muslin and a huge pair of moustaches and a shawl with a fringe is folded on his shoulder like a plaid. The horse's mane and tail, the fringe and the turban blow away behind him as he gallops through the forest and the strangeness and the excitement and gallantry of him seems to sum up for us our day.

We leave the car at the village and, as we walk home to Sabrina, we have to take three coolies to carry home our parcels.

> I was five. The next day I was six. I did go to Darjeeling. It is a town on a mountain. I went up

> there and I saw the Snows more near than I have ever seen them. They are great white, great white, mountains and Mt. Everest is the highest in the world. The houses were all colours and the people were hill people and the hill ladies wore aprons with stripes on them. The market place had lots of jewellery and there was a shop for selling bottles. There were no cars, only ponies and rickshaws and it is very cold in Darjeeling; you have to wear winter coats and still you are cold.
>
> Essay by Rafael.

For the winter, Ayah has bought a black velvet bodice fitting and buttoned with full black sleeves. It makes a very good shape. With it she wears a skirt, white and starched, and a red plaid woollen head-shawl that she retires into when she is cold.

Rafael. And if your legs are cold, Ayah, why not have a black velvet petticoat as well?

The colours on Ayah are exquisite with her black hair and eyes, her gentle gold-brown face and the gold rings in her ears.

Old Sol stood up from where he had been comfortably lying asleep in the sun and stretched himself. His head reared; his back arched and his eyeballs glared for a moment; then he fell over on his side, and died.

I was sitting at my desk writing. He did not make a sound, but I looked up and saw him. It had not been a few seconds. He looked exactly as he had before, asleep in the sun, but he was dead.

On my knees beside him I could not believe it. His coat was warm from the sun, but his heart was still and his neck rolled as I lifted him.

I called Kokil and showed him. Kokil looked down on Sol lying at his feet and his moustaches moved. Then he went quickly behind the door and I heard him weeping.

Old Sol. Part of my days. Part of me.

We bury him near the arbour, under the lemon trees.

Rafael. What shall we put on his grave? A stone? *She thinks for a moment and then thinks better.* It should be pansies for a pekinese.

Today again at the Viewpoint I notice very much the different grades of blue in the sky; it is a deep, a summer blue up in the dome, pale on the north above the snows, and behind us it does not seem to have any horizon, the mountains are too near and too high and cut it off in a mist the colour of forget-me-nots.

I read to Rafael and she reads to me. I read to her about

China, which is filling my thoughts and about which she already knows a great deal. We then discuss: why the Chinese are yellow; the poverty and age of the new water-man; why the people here think Kanchenjunga is a God; and whether you should wash clothes in water that is full of GERMS.

The Sikkim snows are very beautiful and are getting more wintry, more streaked with snow than I have ever seen them. Our weather must break soon and then it will be cold.

Ears asks for leave to go to Sikkim and show himself to his relations. I ask him to wait. It seems that something is stirring out of this solitude for me too. I hold off the moment as long as possible, I do not want it, but unmistakably it has stirred. Soon Ears may be at liberty to go.

I ask for a list of the servants' children for the Christmas tree. On it is written that Baju has a child of six and a child of three.

'You mean *grandchildren*.'

But they are Baju's children and Baju, on questioning, is eighty-three.

I think, if I want to affirm anything, of what I believe, of what I have to say, it is a belief in the individual. I believe in the individual who recognises brotherhood and yet retains his individuality, being filled with it; and I think this is what I mean by God, God or force or spirit; God in man and in all things living; God as life.

I believe in individuality and brotherhood and I believe in freedom; not the freedom that eschews duty, but the freedom of the spirit, free from its preoccupation with materialism. After this time of solitude I can see how preoccupied with material things I was. I want the material side of life so simplified and disciplined that the spirit can be free. I can appreciate the material things, very much enjoy them, and yet eschew them as much as I like.

I am strongly against any societies or sects or institutions. As soon as you form a society you form a limitation and growth should not be limited, the growth of the spirit that distinguishes man from the animals should not be limited; granted of course that many men are merely fine animals. All the greatest thinkers have been independents and renegades and revolutionaries; though they may have needed to go through the discipline of church and sect as they needed to go through school, they discarded them when the time was ripe. If man grows he should pass beyond this need and recognise his own world and the God in himself, his glory and his power; and to do this he should spend a great deal of time alone.

I should like to force everyone from their very beginnings to spend some time alone. How I believe in that.

THERE IS A curious complete silence at Chinglam, unbroken by a letter or a telegram or a telephone call. It seems to fit this Christmas, which is odd, as surely at Christmas the posts ought to be full. There is nothing; no one; no arrival. It should be melancholy, but it is not. It has a quality of enchantment.

W. and M. have gone to camp as have all the other Europeans on the gardens near; there is now no one of our own kind nearer than Darjeeling, eighteen miles away.

The weather has changed too. There are grey still clouds lit by the sun behind them and this light turns the side of the hills to a blue that I always think of when I think of Mary's mantle. The jasmine in the garden is covered with small yellow stars that seem to hold the light, and in the house life moves on in a rhythm that is barely perceptible because it is so quiet. Anyone watching the house would see only slight comings and goings: the white pony trotting out to the post with a few Christmas parcels; Rafael and Sabrina going for a walk by themselves, their heads bobbing in the tea; the dogs running out and scattering and running in again, and me, coming out to pick a bunch of sweet-peas.

There is no word, no sound. The river has died to a thread that makes only the thread of a whisper; even the dew lies long and steadily on the grass; there is no brilliance of sun to dry it.

Coming home before dark.

Rafael. That star follows us as if we were the three wise men.

That is seasonable.

The garden-boy has a baby and the baby has a boil on its buttock; the whole of one side is swollen into an immense cruel boil. I send for the Doctor Babu.

Doctor Babu. Of what is the use? The skin of buttock is very coarse, it will not burst of itself. The only cure is to cut.

'Then cut it.'

The Doctor Babu smiles. That they will not permit.

I speak to the garden-boy. I call Rafael and show him the tiny scar over her eyebrow and tell him it has come from just such a boil and how we cut it to relieve it and how it healed and was cured. He looks at it as if his very soul would rake out from Rafael what happened and then he agrees. The boil is cut and though he breathes and shakes he does not interfere. He carries away the baby at last and it is asleep against his shoulder and the back of its trousers that are cut away as all sensible Nepali babies have their trousers cut away, shows a bottom proudly swathed in bandages and cotton-wool. The Doctor Babu puts away his lance and mounts his pony. 'This is uncommon, I assure you,' says the Doctor Babu.

THINKING OF CHRISTMAS; it has always worried me before and this is the first Christmas I have had as I want it. The Christmases I have known have been gross with fattening and killing. Christ should not be feasted like that and it is Christ's feast; his day. Why not feast him with beauty and moderation, an essence like a poem of festival? At Chinglam ours is turning into that.

There is no one here but the children and me. Rafael is immersed in preparations, she had been for days; not one of them is for herself and she is an intensely possessive, self-engrossed child.

We go up to gather moss and make a crib; it is very simple, made of half a basket to shape a cave standing in moss, and the floor of the cave is sprinkled with clean sawdust. Only the animals are in it now; it waits for the holy family to come into it tonight, which is Christmas Eve.

We go out with the woodcutter and cut down the tree; he does not like this; he does not understand what it is for and he sulks; he does not want to stand waiting while we choose the tree we all like; *he* wants to cut down the one on the edge of the thicket that will give him the least trouble. It is misshapen on one side and we discard it and choose a shapely slender tree while he waits leaning sulkily on his axe. He cuts our tree down and carries it home for us and dumps it on the verandah. I explain that I want it planted in a coolie basket in the middle of the drawing-room floor. His expression says clearly: 'She is not only unnecessary, but mad as well.' He plants it and goes.

We put boughs of cherry round the basket because they are so beautiful with their bright green leaves and bright red leaf stems. We dress the tree in the afternoon; on it we have hundreds of candles, a very little tinsel, icicles and a star; it is not to be a mass of gaudiness that looks more like Woolworth's than a living tree.

We sit down by the fire and look at it. Two stockings are ready side by side, W.'s stockings lent for the occasion.

Rafael, with a deep sigh. Now we are quite ready. We only have to go to bed.

But I feel treacherous and worried. I do not tell Rafael, I do not tell Sabrina, but nothing is ready. On a shelf in my cupboard is a pile of wrapping-paper and tinsel string and labels—and nothing to wrap in them. Nothing has come. None of the things I ordered, no presents from relations or friends. We seem to have been forgotten. I have written, telegraphed; the post is still empty. The children do not know that anything is even slightly wrong, they have complete faith, in me and other people and they deliriously run and hide themselves at post time so that they shall not see what is not there. *Have* we been forgotten? Could even ——— have forgotten them? Even W. and M.? Have the shops gone deaf? I have no means of getting to Darjeeling. I cannot conjure Christmas out of the mountain.

Rafael goes again to look at the parcels we have tied for the servants' children, and again to look under her pillow, where there is a parcel for Sabrina and another for me, which I have known about for weeks. They ran to look at the tree, to shake out again their stockings. Every time they meet on the verandah or in the rooms, they hug each other. Still I sit by the fire and say nothing. This is war time, there are hundreds of children with nothing at all, but I look at Rafael's bubbling face and Sabrina's serene in expectation of the new doll she has been longing for, and I do not know what to do.

Then Monbad brings me a folded note. It is from the postmaster at Rungli-Rungliot:

Please to send your mens because there is too much weight in parcels for you here.

And here is also a man from Rungolo, from W. and M., with a basket full of sweet-peas and two red watering- cans and two chocolate Father Christmases.

Rafael. It has begun.

AND AT SIX o'clock on Christmas morning Ayah, Mrs. Ears, comes softly into my room and presses my feet when she sees I am awake, but does not speak. She kneels and puts a handful of shavings into the fireplace and goes out and brings in a little shovel of red-hot coals. She kneels again and lights the shavings and blows gently with a sound like the wind in the chimney and I see the red reflection of the flames leap up and catch gleams in her ear-rings. The room slowly fills with firelight, red on the white-washed walls, and I lie and watch it and smell the scent of the burning logs and the scent of the roses as they grow warm in the vase. Outside the garden is still dark and there are stars.

Ayah. Lie still and I will bring you some tea. Lie still a little longer before the babas come in.

She presses my feet again between her hands and goes out. It is delicious to lie with the warmth lapping over me while the cool darkness is outside the window.

I worked far into the night yesterday, but now the cupboard door is locked firmly on the secrets, and some of them would not fit in and had to be piled on the top. There are letters and cards and telegrams waiting in the next room where the tree stands ready, and a wooden Joseph and Mary stand each side of the only Holy Child I could find, a small porcelain one meant for a christening cake. Rafael sang 'Once in Royal David's City' which she chose because of her eternal interest in kings and queens, and Sabrina sang:

> O Christmas tree, O Christmas tree,
> How faithful are your leaves.
> You grow with summer's fairest rose
> And with the winter's bitter snows.

O Christmas tree, O Christmas tree,
How faithful are your leaves.

I lie after Ayah has left me. Not one of the dogs have lifted their noses from their willow-pattern cushions, but in the stable I can hear Peter blow down his nose and Whitelegs answer him. My cock crows; he does not know that he was fattened to be eaten today, only I could not bear it and left him alive to crow. He crows and from the children's bedroom comes a first faint rustle, but for a little longer, I can lie between the starlight and the firelight, in the peace of this Christmas early morning.

Dear . . . .
We did cut down our own Christmas tree and we were all alone at Christmas, but we did not mind. We did put Jesus in the crib because he was born wasn't he? and morning was Christmas Day and we did find our stockings *full*. . . .

We are having such a funny party, all the servants children to come, twenty-four children and all to have presents. If we don't go now it won't be ready; if we do go now it will be ready, so I think we had better go.'

Letter from Rafael.

WITH THE SERVANTS today, it has been the finding of two wells of liking and trust. They are maddening servants and I am a maddening mistress: I like things very differently from the English they have known and served, and I leave money about and lose my keys. Today it is all forgotten.

Their glory and wonder at the tree is a revelation. Whole families come. They sit on the floor with their faces turned up to the light of the candles. There are smothered exclamations from the women, 'Ah-ma-ma-ma-ma-ma-ma!'

The woodcutter comes. He does not take in, at once, that this—*this*—is the tree he unwillingly cut down. Very slowly he understands. In his face is wonder and stupefaction and wonder and shame, and suddenly I see him wipe his eyes on his finger. I turn away quickly to the tree and he turns his face to look outside. After a little while, when he thinks no one notices, he comes and stands beside me and with the same finger touches the tree.

'Is it beautiful now?'

But beautiful and ugly have not separated themselves for him.

Woodcutter, softly. Did it cost a lot of money, your honour?

All the children behave in a very stately way; they are barefoot, but heavily dressed about the head, the boys in hats, the girls in shawls and hair ribbons and ear-rings; some of the small ones wear their head shawls crossed under their chins and tied round their necks with the two ends sticking up behind; they look like rabbits.

Monbad's sister comes with his baby tied on her back; they both have refined delicate faces like his; the delicacy is not only in the family face. After the tree the mother and wife come to see me; they did not come to the tree, as this is a visit to *me* and not to gain pleasure. They bring me eggs and roses. I invite them in to see the tree and light the candles again for them; they are afraid to step on the blue carpet and dust their feet and stand with their toes curled carefully away from it. I see them shyly touch Sabrina's hair and again there is that soft exclamation, 'Ah-ma-ma-ma!'

December 26th.

It is still silent. Still mist.

Out of the mist that walls us, today there suddenly comes a whole flight of minivets. They are not much larger than humming-birds, some are completely scarlet and some are yellow. They settle on a bare tree and the tree looks as if it had come out in winter berries. They do not make a sound; they only fly in circles and spirals of colour, in the grey sky.

December 28th.

I feel the year running out. There is still the silence, though today the mist has gone, but this quiet must break soon. I am expectant of it. This is the pause, the holding of breath, before something begins. Perhaps something will begin in the new year; meanwhile I am clinging to the old, drawing out the days though they seem to draw, of themselves, into length.

We go up to the Viewpoint and it feels as if this were the last time. All the way up, after the soaking mists, the banks are very green and full of moss and blue flowers that have spread down from the bamboo wood; they are still wet, liquid blue. Above them the cherry trees are in sun, all their leaves fingering—yes, fingering, with bright green fingers—the air and the wind.

It is cold and warm together: that keeps my body awake and alive, it does not know which is coming, a warm wind or a cold, sun balmy from the bank or chilled from the expanse to the snows.

I like the snows best when they are more blue than white, and streaked with snow; they are blue this morning all the way round from Sikkim to Kabru, the same blue as the flowers.

As I canter softly up on Peter to the last stretch of the path, a barking deer jumps off our seat at the Point and runs into the tea.

I wait for Rafael to catch me up and I stand by Peter and he curves his neck round me, looking to see if she is coming. His neck is short and white and solid like the rest of him;

he is really like the palfrey on a crest, his tail streams on the wind and his whole body gleams with whiteness. I notice again his thick stubbly white eyelashes. He whinnies when he sees the brown and white patches of Whitelegs coming and she answers and bustles towards him through the tea.

AYAH TELLS THE children how she and the Ears family will walk to Sikkim, getting colder and colder, more away from anyone, more wild.

Ayah. And we shall sleep in the jungle and we shall have only one light.

Rafael comes to tell me, trembling with pity, and tears.

'Tell Ayah I envy her. Sikkim is one of the most beautiful places in the world.'

THE DAYS ARE breaking up here. Baju has finished himself. In a fit of drunkenness last night he set fire to the straw beside the stable. The servants and I spent half the night putting it out, digging down the bank on top of it. We were black and choked with smoke; Kokil girded up his dhoti, his long flowing nether draperies, and stepped down into the middle of it. They all thought it rather a joke, but I and Ears and the ponies were very much alarmed. We have had no rain for two months and there were dry leaves and wisps of straw all over the garden and the wind was blowing towards the house. The stable is only built of bamboo and thatch, and when I came out and found them, the flames were rising up beside it. Baju was too drunk to come, or turn out the coolies. I had to telephone to W.

This morning Baju is dismissed after fifty-three years' service on the garden. He will get a pension, but it is the loss of face that is bitter for him. I do not think either W. or I could have acted in any other way; he has been drunk for weeks now, sometimes gently and sometimes badly. I feel as I did about his marigolds, but there is no doubt that it has strengthened my hand here at Chinglam.

Monbad. He disobeyed the Memsahib, he did not come when she called and you see, he is sent away.

I do not come into it at all. He has been sent away for imperilling garden property that is, officially, under his care, even when I am the tenant of it.

It is extraordinary not to see him come trembling to give me his salaam. The new chowkidar is walking busily about, looking at the flowers as if he is determined to account for every leaf.

December 30th.

I wake to a violent day. After the stillness there is a violent cold wind sweeping across the garden and sweeping the mist into black clouds. Down the path from the Saddle after breakfast comes a green khaki figure, slowly slowly creeping, with an umbrella that it is too windy for him to hold. I know him. He is the Rungli-Rungliot telegraph peon.

I know, too, what it is before I open the envelope. We are to go.

December 31st.

In the garden, this last day of the year, there are a few, very few, of my snapdragons out. They are dark red ones and if there had been more of them they would have balanced, beautifully, the cornflowers. I walk round Chinglam and I am begging: 'Don't be too beautiful now. Don't make me love you any more than I need.'

I wonder what traces of me the next assistant to come here will find? Perhaps a party of refugees will come and wipe them all out. Perhaps W. will send no assistant to live here again. Perhaps we are the last and the house will be empty.

It will be empty now. I am both glad and sad that no one is to come after us; no one to inherit the pool in the stream, and the glade and my path on the Saddle and the place under the lemon trees where I work and, perhaps most of all, the Viewpoint and the walk under the cherry trees and the mound where the prayer flags are and the small house. No one has found them before; W. and M. do not know them. Perhaps no one will find them again.

There is no sunset, only the sky goes grey; pale grey in the sky, dark grey in the clouds. It is very gentle and that suits Chinglam. The trees are a queer colour, half olive and half black, and the stars when they come out look extra bright because of the gentleness around them. I notice the white roses.

Comfort comes up and puts her paw on my knee as I sit on the rock above the drive. She divines that I am sad. I am more sad than I can say.

Things I have started and of which I shall not see the fruit.

The snapdragons, poppies, lemon verbenas, lettuces, oranges and chillies.

The servants' manners.

The settings of eggs.

The altering of the stream and the glade.

Whitelegs fattening.

The new bathrooms W. has promised to build.

Things I have hated and things I have loved.

I hated:

Washing my hair myself.

A sordid bathroom with mould on the washing-stand.

The misery of the pack-ponies.

The age telegrams take and the waiting for letters.

Flies.

Not being able to understand the coolies' language.

The smell of the pack-pony urine.

The drum.

The solitude.

I loved:

The solitude.

The lemon trees and the smell of their leaves.

The singing of the coolies.

The presents of pineapples and flowers and eggs and milk.

The garden.

The wood floors and wood fires.

The wild begonias and poinsettias and the millet when it is green and the flowers of the pink crop.

The roving camps of Bhutias and Tibetans.

The effect that Chinglam had on Rafael and Sabrina and the getting to know them better.

The servants.

The prayer flags.

Everything to do with tea.

The wild cherry trees.

The bamboo plumbing.

The walk on the Saddle and the view from it.

The ponies.

The . . . but there were so many things I loved.

THIS BOOK SHOULD smell of lemon leaves. The last thing I do is to pick some and put them in the pages; they will die, but the scent of them, whenever I smell it again, wherever I find it, will mean to me always, Chinglam.